Gothic Architecture
and its Meanings 1550–1830

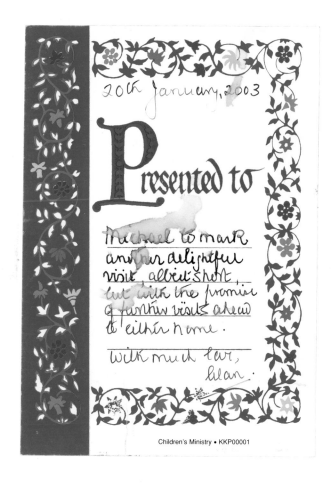

20th January, 2003

Presented to

Michael to mark
another delightful
visit, albeit short,
but with the promise
of further visits ahead
to either home.

with much love,
Alan.

Children's Ministry • KKP00001

Gothic Architecture

and its Meanings 1550–1830

Edited by

Michael Hall

Spire Books Ltd
in association with the Georgian Group

Published by
Spire Books Ltd
PO Box 2336
Reading RG4 5WJ

This book has its origins in a symposium organised by Michael Hall for the Georgian Group on October 28, 2000. The editor and publisher would like to thank Neil Burton, former Director of the Georgian Group, and Robert Bargery, its present Director, for their help in realising this publication.

Publication of this book was assisted by generous grants from the Marc Fitch Fund and the Georgian Group.

CIP data:
A catalogue record for this book is available from the British Library
ISBN 0 9543615 0 4

Designed and produced by John Elliott
Text set in Adobe Bembo

Printed by Alden Group Ltd, Osney Mead, Oxford OX2 0EF

Front & back cover photographs:
Arbury Hall, Warwickshire, 'one of the finest examples of the early Gothic Revival in England – some may say *the* finest, and the finest in England of course implies any-where.'
Nikolaus Pevsner and Alexandra Wedgwood, *The Buildings of England: Warwickshire* (Harmondsworth, 1966), p. 67.

Contents

Introduction

Introduction

Michael Hall

IN 1872 Charles Eastlake, the 36-year-old secretary of the RIBA, published *A History of the Gothic Revival*. The first sustained historical account of the Revival, it was published at the last moment that the story it told could be unquestioningly positive, a fact one could not guess from the triumphalist nature of its conclusion. The final church Eastlake describes is G. F. Bodley's St John in Tue Brook, Liverpool, which had been opened the year before the book appeared. It was not, Eastlake said, for its architectural merits alone that he was singling it out. In the painted decoration of its interior, he wrote, and in particular in Charles Eamer Kempe's mural of the Tree of Life over the chancel arch 'the genuine grace of Mediaeval art seems at length to have been reached. In the architecture which it decorates no appreciable inferiority, whether of design or execution, to the type selected for imitation, can be discerned.'[1]

In other words, Bodley's church represents the conclusion to which the Revival had been working since the antiquaries of the 17th century first began to examine the relics of England's medieval past, where Eastlake begins his story. It is often assumed that he skimps and compresses the early history of the Revival in order to throw into relief the achievements of his own time - every reader of the book recalls his contempt for Batty Langley and patronising praise of Horace Walpole - but he devotes eight of his 20 chapters, a good deal more than a third of the book, to the Gothic Revival before Pugin, and he makes a serious attempt to view the early part of the movement in its historic context. Unlike the ecclesiological propagandists for Gothic in the 1840s and 1850s, who had emphasised solely the differences between, for example, the Gothic of Christopher Wren and that of Pugin, Eastlake reminds us of the continuities. Although, like all his contemporaries, he judged St Mary Aldermary and St Dunstan-in-the-East by the standards of medieval design, and found them 'melancholy examples of Gothic art', he reminds us that 'any examples which date from such a period become valuable

Opposite:
St John,
Tue Brook,
Liverpool 1867-70,
opened 1871
by G. F. Bodley
(*National Monuments Record*).

links in the history of its revival'.[2] In other words, the story
he tells is of a largely unbroken, although occasionally inter-
rupted, progression in recapturing a full understanding of
medieval architecture in order to recreate it to serve the
needs of the present. It is an understanding of the Gothic
Revival that has failed to find much favour, largely because
no writer since Eastlake's time has shared his assumption that
the progress of the Gothic Revival was an unfolding triumph.

  The belief that the Revival had in fact been a failure

was already current within a decade of the appearance of Eastlake's book. It was articulated most persuasively by Richard Norman Shaw in a letter to John Dando Sedding of 1882 which has especial force, given that both men were such distinguished practitioners of the style. Looking back on the history of the Revival, Shaw writes that

> to all intents and purposes a new style was revived, dug up, call it what you will. Every feature of that style was in direct antagonism to every tradition of work then existing ... and for all practical purposes the style dug up might just as well have been Chinese or Egyptian and we have struggled on with that style from that day till this, between 40 & 50 years now. We have done it in perfect good faith, there can be no doubt, but that it is in any sense whatever a living art, I cannot see.[3]

In other words, Gothic, a dead art, was to be left to antiquaries, who, as the 19th century progressed, steadily lost any sense of common purpose with architects.

Such attitudes at the very top of the architectural profession make it clear why two generations passed before Eastlake's work had a successor. In 1928 Kenneth Clark published his first book, *The Gothic Revival*. Because it stops with the death of Pugin - something that Clark readily admitted made a full appreciation of the Gothic Revival impossible - it is often assumed that his sympathies were with the earlier phases of the subject. To some degree this is true: Clark influentially identified the 18th-century taste for Gothic as rococo in spirit and emphasised its literary sources and romantic, associative qualities. Yet he was every bit as harsh as Eastlake in his assessment of Strawberry Hill, albeit for entirely the opposite reasons: 'Bad art flourishes in every epoch,' he wrote, 'but art may be healthily or unhealthily bad, and Strawberry was bad in a peculiarly ominous way. Walpole's taste seems to have found satisfaction in just those things which were to bring about the collapse of architecture in the nineteenth century. He introduced a romantic style, and instead of using his borrowed forms freely, as the Renaissance used Classical forms, he insisted on copying them. If his Gothic shows a little more style than Gilbert

Scott's, it is because he was an incompetent copyist, and a little eighteenth-century feeling crept into his medievalism.'[4]

In other words, Eastlake's approach has been accepted in intellectual terms – Walpole is of interest as a stage in an unfolding story – but his judgment is inverted. Because, in Clark's eyes, the 19th-century Gothic Revival was a failure, albeit an historically interesting one, anything that Walpole did that could be understood as contributing to its development must be condemned. For Clark, no less than for Eastlake, attitudes to the 19th-century Gothic Revival governed his understanding of the movement in the 18th century.

In the meantime, appreciation of Georgian Gothic was taken forward in unexpected ways. The 1920s witnessed a revival of interest in 18th-century architecture and design that in aesthetic terms had long roots, back to the beginnings of the Queen Anne movement in the 1860s, but was given a

new fillip in the post-war period by country-house owners. The decline in the political influence of the aristocracy, which had accelerated in the 1870s, had undermined much that the Gothic Revival had stood for – an ideal of landed power based on long family traditions and a sense of a social hierarchy appointed by God. In the 1920s, after a swift and total revolt against Victorian culture, this was replaced by the idea of a hierarchy of taste, with the Classical values represented by 18th-century art and design at its pinnacle. Gothic, which was so closely implicated with 19th-century ideals, fitted rather uneasily into this, but as Clark suggests – although I am not sure whether he had any direct influence – an understanding of 18th-century Gothic as rococo in spirit made it possible to appreciate it in its own terms, and not as a precursor of Victorian Gothic. To spell Gothick with a 'k', which in the 19th century had been a mark of contempt, now came to denote a style which was appreciated for being light, frivolous, witty and even slightly naughty. So influential is this view that it is still, 80 years later, widely accepted, and most standard works on the history of architecture go to some lengths to emphasise the differences between the Gothic Revival in the 18th and 19th centuries. The former, we are often told, is the most enjoyable part of the Gothic Revival because it does not make the mistake of its 19th-century successor of attempting too seriously to look like medieval architecture.

Above and opposite: Details of Rex Whistler's decoration of the drawing room at Mottisfont Abbey, Hampshire, 1938-9 (*Country Life Picture Library*).

This was an approach to Georgian Gothic that almost by accident was reinforced by the distinction between Gothic survival and Gothic Revival. Eastlake and Clark had both been alive to that distinction, but it was opened up for modern architectural history by a highly influential essay by Sir Howard Colvin, which appeared in the *Architectural Review* in 1948.[5] To clarify his forensic examination of a group of masons building churches in a Gothic style in the 18th century he distinguished Gothic Revival from survival by using Gothic with a 'k' for the former. Although this essay suggested how historians could distinguish those buildings in which Gothic had been a matter of conscious choice, most simply rested content with a distinction between 'real' Gothic ('Gothic') and its Georgian 'imitation' ('Gothick'), without following up Sir Howard's invitation to ask why architects

Garden pavilion at the Hunting Lodge, Dogmersfield, Hampshire by John Fowler. (*Country Life Picture Library*).

and masons chose to build in the style.

18th-century Gothic had its own 'Gothick' revival, which produced such exquisite masterpieces as Rex Whistler's decoration in 1938-9 of the drawing room at Mottisfont Abbey for Mr and Mrs Gilbert Russell, and remained popular well into the 1950s, with the work of interior decorators, most notably perhaps John Fowler's work for his old partner Nancy Lancaster at Haseley Court in Oxfordshire, and at his own country house, the Hunting Lodge, an 18th-century Gothic pavilion in the park at Dogmersfield in Hampshire.[6] It was an approach to 18th-century design that was enshrined in good scholarship as well as numerous popular books right up to the present day, most notably Terence Davis's enjoyable and comprehensive account *The Gothick Taste*, published in 1974. Few historians now use the term 'Gothic-with-a-k' without inverted commas, since it is anachronistic, but the term should perhaps be preserved to describe a minor but enchanting style of the 20th century.[7]

It may be thought rather cheeky to link the names of Rex Whistler and John Fowler with that of the author of the most influential history of British architecture published in the past century, but Sir John Summerson did not feel it necessary to advance the understanding of the Gothic Revival in the 18th century much beyond theirs. His *Architecture in Britain 1530-1830*, first published in 1953, has little to say about Gothic architecture. It may be thought reasonable that any account of British architecture in this period should treat Gothic design as a minor sideshow, but since Summerson did not call his book 'Classical Architecture in Britain 1530-1830' it is a clear imbalance to have devoted so little space to the subject - just 18 pages out of the 565 of main text in the

current edition[8] – before the arrival of the Picturesque movement in the penultimate chapter makes the subject unavoidable. It is not that Summerson exactly disapproved of the Gothic Revival before 1830, for he writes about it with interest, but he clearly did not think there was much importance in what he calls 'the flimsy decorative equivalents for Gothic which were to persist throughout the eighteenth century and only to disappear under the censure of the Victorian Gothic school itself'.[9] The principal house he illustrates in addition to Strawberry Hill is Lacock Abbey, where he emphasises that 'the whole thing was done (as the surviving correspondence makes clear) as a light-hearted extravaganza'.[10] Strawberry Hill, he writes, was less influential in terms of the Gothic Revival than previous writers had assumed, but it was an important landmark in the Picturesque movement.

Hall, Lacock Abbey, Wiltshire, by Sanderson Miller, 1754-6. (*Country Life Picture Library*).

With histories of architecture that focus on style, there is a tendency to treat architectural styles as Platonic paradigms, somehow existing independently of the buildings in which they are manifested, and indeed Summerson, like so many scholars of his time, refused to accept that 18th-century

The Library,
Strawberry Hill,
Middlesex,
1754 (*Country Life
Picture Library*).

Gothic is real Gothic. It may now be thought self-evident that we must adjust our definition of a style to accommodate all its manifestations, but to Summerson, as to Eastlake, 18th-century Gothic was mere imitation. 'Real Gothic' is usually stated to be medieval, but the underlying assumption is surely that the 19th-century Gothic Revival is the norm against which Georgian architects are to be judged.

The clue to Summerson's attitude lies, I suspect, in his struggle to come to terms with Victorian architecture, which, in common with Clark, he saw as a failure. Like Clark, and like so many other writers, his approach to the Gothic Revival before 1830 was skewed by his attitude to its later, 19th-century manifestation. He was fascinated by Victorian design, but like most of his generation found it a challenge to understand or to like, a challenge that resulted in a series of influential essays ranging from 'William Butterfield; or, the Glory of Ugliness', which appeared in 1949,[11] to his lecture 'The Evaluation of Victorian Architecture: The Problem of Failure', published in 1971.[12] The validity or otherwise of his arguments is not the point here: what matters is that Summerson's belief that something went badly wrong with British architecture in the 1830s and 1840s encouraged an

intellectual *cordon sanitaire* between 18th- and 19th-century studies. This made a complete understanding of the Gothic Revival so hard to achieve, for it overlooked any sense of the continuity between, for example, Henry Keene and George Gilbert Scott, which Clark had sensed, but of which he had disapproved. The 1830s have become a moat which surprisingly few scholars cross with ease, perpetuating a gulf evident in such divisions in architectural history and conservation as that between the Georgian Group and the Victorian Society.

Summerson's account of the Gothic Revival has been deepened by much scholarly activity in the past 20 years, with, perhaps most notably, work on the medievalising designs of Wren and Hawksmoor and their circle, and the Gothic architecture of William Kent, which has revealed how much 'keeping in keeping' was a powerful motive for much Gothic design.[13] Much attention has focused on the place of Gothic in garden design and garden and park buildings, emphasising that such structures were often the focus for architectural experimentation, but in the process perhaps tending to reinforce a perception of the style as marginal.

Arbury Hall, Warwickshire (*Country Life Picture Library*).

Many of these new interests were evident in the Georgian Group's previous symposium on the Gothic Revival – Gothick was then spelled with a 'k' – in 1983.[14] Perhaps the most radical reassessment has been Eileen Harris's of Batty Langley, which rediscovered an unsuspected intellectual context for his work in freemasonry;[15] a comparable analysis of a later architect and writer is J. Mordaunt Crook's study of John Carter.[16] That sort of contextual history is still relatively rare in 17th- and 18th-century architectural studies, with one major exception, the growing interest in what architecture reveals about attitudes to the past; in other words, antiquarianism. This is doubtless in part a reaction to the historical philosophy of Modernism with its stress on progress and obedience to the *zeitgeist* and in part a reaction to the argument by so many cultural historians of the 1970s and 1980s that Britain had ceased to be a forward-looking country and was inhabiting what they called a heritage culture.

There is now great interest in the way that architects and patrons deliberately set out to quote or imitate the architecture of the past. There have been some eye-opening arguments, such as Mark Girouard's analysis of Burghley as a consciously medievalising building,[17] and it is a subject that Giles Worsley takes up in this volume, in his discussion of Vanbrugh's interest in historic English architecture. The use of old forms and styles to emphasise a family's history has been a fruitful theme in recent country-house studies. It may be clear in the saloon at Audley End, for example, that Sir John Griffin Griffin set out in the 1760s to create an interior that would proclaim his family's ancestry, by adding Jacobean-style and Gothic plasterwork to form a setting for a sequence of portraits of his ancestors;[18] it was less clear that a house such as Cotehele in Cornwall is a patchwork of 16th- and 17th-century interior design overlaid, as John Cornforth has shown, by an 18th-century remodelling designed to emphasise that this was an ancient house.[19]

This new approach has made it easier to accept that Gothic Revival architecture embodies ideas about the past. Yet until recently architectural historians have been surprisingly reluctant to ask what those ideas might consist of, over and beyond 'keeping in keeping' or families asserting their

ancestry.[20] There is no doubt that Gothic could in some cases carry political implications. Yet it was not until the 1990s, notably for example in David Stewart's controversial study of the political meanings of Gothic park buildings in the form of ruins, that such ideas were seriously addressed,[21] and it was not until Chris Brooks's history of the Gothic Revival, published in 1999, that such ideas featured in any sustained way in a general survey of the subject.[22]

To focus for the moment on the first half of the 18th century, Gothic was clearly the architecture of opposition at a time when political legitimacy was a matter of intense and sometimes dangerous debate. The most celebrated example of this is James Gibbs's Gothic Temple at Stowe, designed for Lord Cobham and built in 1744-8 as the climax of his garden's ideological programme.[23] It was designed to make clear his beliefs as the leader of the party that had broken with the Whigs as a result of Robert Walpole's government introducing excise duty in 1733. Cobham and his allies rallied around the opposition figure of Frederick, Prince of Wales, who proclaimed himself to be another Alfred, the defender of the nation's ancient liberties against overweening autocracy. As such, he was celebrated in James Thomson and Thomas Arne's masque *Alfred*, first performed in 1740, just four years before Cobham built the Gothic Temple, which he called 'Saxon'. It was surrounded by statues of the Saxon deities and has a vault painted with the heraldry of Cobham's supposed Saxon ancestors.

This was an assertion that Cobham and his allies were the defenders of the true, that is the Gothic, constitution. That assertion helps resolve the question of how Gothic could have been capable of bearing clear political meanings despite being co-opted by political opponents. How, it has often been asked, could contemporaries understand Gothic in political terms when it was so central to the architectural endeavours of both Horace Walpole, the son of the greatest of all Whig prime ministers, and Roger Newdigate, builder of Arbury Hall in Warwickshire, who not merely voted with the Tories, but who had secret Jacobite sympathies, proclaimed in the Stuart roses and stars of the stained glass in the dining room at Arbury?[24] The answer must be that Gothic was a forum for that struggle over Hanoverian legitimacy which broke out into open revolt in 1715 and 1745. Both Walpole and Newdigate were arguing that their political beliefs were validated by ancient authority. As far as I am aware, Newdigate only once uses the word Gothic in all his copious letters, diaries and other writings, but it refers not to architectural form but to the nature of the British constitution.[25] That link was something which Walpole

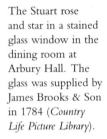

would never concede to somebody he felt was disloyal to the Hanoverian cause.

The Stuart rose and star in a stained glass window in the dining room at Arbury Hall. The glass was supplied by James Brooks & Son in 1784 (*Country Life Picture Library*).

The extent of that disloyalty in British society as a whole has been a matter of intense debate between what it is not too fanciful to see as a Tory/Whig split in contemporary historians of the 18th century. In 1985 Jonathan Clark

Dining room, Arbury Hall, Warwickshire (*Country Life Picture Library*).

launched a major historiographical debate with his book provocatively titled *English Society 1688-1832: Ideology, Social Structure and Political Practice during the Ancien Régime*.[26] A passionate attack on what he called 'the materialist and teleological Whig–Marxist reductionism of current historical thinking' about the 18th century, he argued that England before the lifting of civil restrictions on non-conformists and Catholics in 1828-9 was 'a confessional state' that deserved the term '*ancien régime*'. Ideology, not economics, was at the centre of his picture of British society, which emphasised its agrarian, aristocratic and religious character rather than the industrialist, middle-class and radical non-conformity which had appealed so much to so many historians in the 1960s and 1970s. It was a picture that helped open up a major debate about the nature of Jacobite belief in early-18th-century England: Clark's approach appeared to support arguments by such historians as Eveline Cruickshanks that, far from being the preserve of a few backwoods Scottish aristocrats, it had permeated opposition politics for half a century.[27]

That argument was challenged by Linda Colley, whose Cambridge PhD thesis on the nature of the opposition to the Whigs in early-18th-century England, published in 1982 as *In Defiance of Oligarchy*, had concluded that loyalty to the Stuarts was a minor and marginal force. The disapproval that she and her followers felt for Jonathan Clark's thesis was summed up in a lecture by her husband, David Cannadine, in 1987 on the future of history in English universities. Agreeing that the subject had recently witnessed the collapse of the Whig model of social history, he asked 'into which part of the contemporary terrain should we choose to engage?' His answer is revealing:

> Several attempts have recently been made. The first is by the new high-political archive-grubbers, whose accounts of brief episodes in the history of seventeenth-, eighteenth- and nineteenth-century England are so myopic as to be almost devoid of any meaning at all. A second is the revived cult of the country house, most recently exemplified in the 'Treasure Houses of Britain' exhibition at Washington, which took a view of the British past at once so snobbish and so unhistorical that it was almost a parody of *Brideshead*

Revisited. A third is to be found in the recent celebration of our country's so-called individualism, which in fact offers a Thatcherite, little England interpretation of Britain's past, but does so only by ignoring most of the available evidence. And a fourth is the new Jacobite interpretation of history, a wilfully perverse celebration of such obscurantist troglodytes as the Young Pretender, the Tractarians and the duke of Windsor, which makes even the embittered splutterings of Hilaire Belloc seem models of balance and wisdom by comparison.[28]

Professor Cannadine's best-known work, *The Decline and Fall of the English Aristocracy*, which appeared in 1990, was to show that there was plenty of life left in the old Whig model of the history of British society. Perhaps the Duke of Windsor does not count for much, but a view of British history which demands that the Tractarians be omitted will make it impossible to understand the story of the Gothic Revival in the 19th century; omitting the Young Pretender as well may cause similar difficulties for the 18th century. It will certainly not help us to understand why Sir Roger Newdigate spent 50 years of his life rebuilding Arbury, in part as a symbolic embodiment of the British constitution. The Kenneth Clark or Summerson portrayal of 18th-century Gothic as rococo in character will not do for the major case of Arbury. There was nothing light, frivolous or theatrical about Newdigate, nor is there about his house. Moreover, Arbury undermines any attempt to reduce the study of the Gothic Revival to the traditions of antiquarianism, since Newdigate was not for most of his life in any sense an antiquary.[29] He also makes it more difficult to portray the Gothic Revival as a series of more-or-less unrelated episodes rather than any sort of continuous tradition.

In his pious, Catholic understanding of Anglicanism and in his belief in historical authority for the hierarchy of British society, Newdigate closely resembles those Tractarian squires and clergymen who were to promote the Gothic Revival so forcefully a generation after his death. In that sense, he looks forward, and makes it clear that too strong a distinction is made between High Church beliefs in the 19th century and in earlier periods. That distinction goes back to the propaganda of the Oxford Movement itself, which sought to portray the 18th-century High Church as ideologically and spiritually inert, a judgement which has only recently been seriously challenged by historians.[30]

Just as importantly, Newdigate also points backwards. It may be a surprise that a Warwickshire squire so outwardly loyal to Church and Crown should have harboured such deep sympathy for the Stuarts, yet it no longer is particularly controversial to assert that a large proportion of the British ruling class found it difficult to accept not only the legitimacy of the Hanoverian succession but also the revolution of 1688. There is moreover something deeply revealing about Newdigate, who sternly resisted Catholic emancipation at home, being profoundly moved by attending a papal mass at St Peter's in 1775: 'Such a throne as that noble church', he wrote, '& such humble adoration can no where else be found'.[31] Is it possible that he had a sense that some essential continuity in British society had been fractured not just in 1688 but at the Reformation itself, and that Gothic was a powerfully symbolic way of reasserting it? That would be a commonplace view in the Anglican High Church of the 19th century, and there is no obvious reason why if it existed then, it should not have been felt in the 18th century - and perhaps in the 17th and 16th centuries as well. Such beliefs have been marginalised by Whig historians in the same way that architectural historians, who tend to be Whigs by temperament, have until recently marginalised the Gothic Revival. Whether there was indeed any serious and sustained engagement between such views of British society and the revival of Gothic architecture over a period of 300 years is one of the issues addressed in this book.

Notes
1 Charles L. Eastlake, *A History of the Gothic Revival* (London, 1872), p. 371.
2 Ibid., p. 35.
3 R. N. Shaw to J. D. Sedding, November 5, 1882 (National Art Library, Victoria and Albert Museum), quoted in Andrew Saint, *Richard Norman Shaw* (New Haven and London, 1976), pp. 217–18.

4 Kenneth Clark, *The Gothic Revival* (second edition, reprinted Harmondsworth, 1964), p. 51.

5 H. M. Colvin, 'Gothic Survival and Gothick Revival', *Architectural Review*, 103 (1948), pp. 91–8, reprinted with revisions in H. M. Colvin, *Essays in English Architectural History* (New Haven and London, 1999), pp. 217–44.

6 These buildings and schemes are illustrated and discussed in John Cornforth, *The Inspiration of the Past: Country House Taste in the Twentieth Century* (London, 1985).

7 Giles Worsley, 'What's in a "K"', *Country Life,* April 21, 1994.

8 John Summerson, *Architecture in Britain 1530-1830* (first edition, Harmondsworth, 1953; I have referred to the 1986 reprint of the seventh edition, Harmondsworth, 1983).

9 Ibid., p. 398.

10 Ibid., pp. 401–2.

11 Published in John Summerson, *Heavenly Mansions and other Essays on Architecture* (London, 1949), pp. 159–76.

12 Published in John Summerson, *Victorian Architecture in England: Four Studies in Evaluation* (New York, 1970, reprinted 1971), pp. 1–18.

13 See the chapter 'The Continuing Gothic Tradition' in Giles Worsley, *Classical Architecture in Britain: The Heroic Age* (New Haven and London, 1995), pp. 175–95, and the references given there.

14 Its proceedings were published by the Georgian Group as *A Gothick Symposium at the Victoria and Albert Museum* (London, 1983).

15 Eileen Harris, 'Batty Langley: A Tutor to Freemasons', *Burlington Magazine* (May, 1977), pp. 327–35; Eileen Harris, assisted by Nicholas Savage, *British Architectural Books and Writers* (Cambridge, 1990), pp. 262–80.

16 J. Mordaunt Crook, *John Carter and the Mind of the Gothic Revival* (London, 1995).

17 Mark Girouard, 'Burghley House, Lincolnshire', *Country Life*, April 23, 1992.

18 John Cornforth, 'Audley End, Essex', *Country Life*, January 3, 1991.

19 John Cornforth, 'Cothele, Cornwall', *Country Life*, February 1 and 8, 1990.

20 See Giles Worsley, op. cit. [note 13], pp. 175–95.

21 David Stewart, 'Political Ruins: Gothic Sham Ruins and the '45', *Journal of the Society of Architectural Historians*, 55 (1996), pp. 400–11.

22 Chris Brooks, *The Gothic Revival* (London, 1999).

23 On Cobham, see George Clarke, 'Grecian Taste and Gothic Virtue: Lord Cobham's Gardening Programme and its Iconography', *Apollo*, 97 (1973), pp. 566-71.

24 Michael Hall, 'Arbury Hall, Warwickshire', *Country Life*, January 7 and 14, 1999.

25 For Newdigate's writings, see A. W. A. White (editor), *The Correspondence of Sir Roger Newdigate* (Dugdale Society, Hertford, 1995); Anthony C. Wood, 'The Diaries of Sir Roger Newdigate 1751-1806', *Transactions of the Birmingham & Warwickshire Archaeological Society*, 78 (1962), pp. 40-54; Peter D. G. Thomas, 'Sir Roger Newdigate's Essays on Party, c.1760', *English Historical Review*, 102 (1987), pp. 394-400.

26 Published by Cambridge University Press in 1985. For an assessment of its impact on the historiography of the 18th century, see Joanna Innes, 'Social History and England's Ancien Régime', *Past & Present*, 115 (1987), pp. 165-200.

27 Eveline Cruickshanks, *Political Untouchables: The Tories and the '45* (London, 1979); Ian R. Christie, 'The Tory Party, Jacobitism and the 'Forty-Five: a Note', *The Historical Journal*, 30, 4 (1987), pp. 921-37; J. C. D. Clark, 'On Moving the Middle Ground: the Significance of Jacobitism in Historical Studies' in Eveline Cruickshanks and Jeremy Black (editors), *The Jacobite Challenge* (Edinburgh, 1988), pp. 177-88.

28 David Cannadine, 'British History: Past, Present – and Future?', *Past & Present*, 116 (1987), pp. 169-91, at pp. 189-90. For J. C. D. Clark's reply, see 'On Hitting the Buffers: the Historiography of England's Ancien Régime', *Past & Present*, 117 (1988), pp. 195-207.

29 See Michael Hall, op. cit. [note 24]; Newdigate did not develop any serious interest in English antiquarian studies until near the end of his life, when in 1797 Daniel Lysons asked him to contribute to his *History of Warwickshire*.

30 Most notably by Peter B. Nockles in *The Oxford Movement in Context: Anglican High Churchmanship 1760-1857* (Cambridge, 1994).

31 Newdigate to John Mordaunt, Rome, April 28, 1775, in White, op. cit. [note 25], p. 204.

1

Interpretations of Medieval Architecture, *c.*1550–*c.*1750

Interpretations of Medieval Architecture, *c.*1550-*c.*1750

Alexandrina Buchanan

FOR A STYLE so evidently allusive, the meanings of Gothic before the 19th century are frustratingly elusive. There is no unequivocal statement of intent by an architect or patron building in a Gothic style. Architectural historians seeking to understand what messages patrons and architects were hoping to convey by their choice of a medieval style are therefore forced to draw inferences from the external evidence of their known political or religious position (which were, of course, rarely unconnected). In this chapter, it is my purpose to explore what potential meanings were available, by looking at the more frequently-expressed attitudes to actual medieval buildings and styles, as recorded in literary, aesthetic and antiquarian sources. The aim is not to be comprehensive but to look in detail at a small number of examples. In so doing, I wish to examine the relationships between literature and architecture in this respect. I hope this discussion may promote further consideration of how (and indeed whether) meanings and associations borne by historical examples relate to those intended for new buildings erected in a reproduction, or approximation, of medieval styles.

An analysis of earlier attitudes towards Gothic is a customary prelude to histories of the 19th-century Gothic Revival. As Michael Hall suggests in the introduction to this volume, the narrative is usually teleological. The normal starting point is the origin of the word 'Gothic'. The account then proceeds with the dissemination of the term, which is often taken to signal the spread of distaste for the style. Next comes a description of the growth of appreciation of medieval buildings, which is seen as an essential prerequisite for its revival by modern builders. *En route* there may be a number of quotations from contemporary authors, taken to reflect these changing attitudes. The background to the Revival is thus depicted as literary: Gothic was first familiarised and approved in texts and only subsequently did it come to be built.[1]

Opposite:
Wayneflete's Tower,
Esher Place, Surrey,
1729-33 (*Lambeth
Palace Library*).

The deliberately provocative title of the present volume – 'Gothic Architecture', not 'Gothic Revival' - proposes that such an account does not tell the whole story. As its authors suggest, there was never a period when Gothic was held in such universal contempt that its forms could not inspire the designers of new buildings. And, perhaps just as significantly, medieval architecture continued to exist: its presence could not be erased from public view. At all levels of society, buildings erected in the Middle Ages continued to serve important functions as houses, churches, educational establishments and other public buildings.

It is thus from the basis of its continued significance that we need to re-evaluate the evidence for attitudes towards the Gothic. The textual evidence for opinions about Gothic or medieval architecture during the period under discussion is relatively scanty and has been much discussed by scholars working in a number of fields. Because the responses appear to conform to a series of types, it has proved tempting to categorise them.[2] The focus is thus placed on definition of meaning, rather than examining how meaning is conveyed. Viewed in this quasi-lexicographical fashion, most statements appear derivative, even clichéd, yet they are often read as though they represent an independent assertion of the views of their user. The speaker may in turn be taken as representative of his or her historical period, political affiliation, religious persuasion or other grouping, in other words as the voice of an interpretive community.[3] Items of discourse may be seen as an expression of the individual, or of society, but of course they may also be no more than an individual's unconsidered reproduction of existing values. Discourse as articulated through texts is yet more problematic, for they too have their own autonomy. When a writer in 1660 employs the same words as a speaker in 1760, do the words mean the same thing? And is the author communicating a personal opinion about medieval architecture, or using the statement as a means by which to locate him or herself within another context, whether it be social, political, religious or aesthetic (or both)? A further problem with the catalogue approach is that by dividing up the types of response and discussing them, one by one, they are made to appear as separate entities, when in fact each is inevitably related to another. It also denies the possibility of alternative responses, which either remained unarticulated or were expressed in conventional terms and thus may not be identified. In short, it encourages us to ignore the context, whether historical, generic or semiotic, of the individual statements.

Such cautionary preliminaries over, this essay too will begin with etymology. Of course, medieval architecture as an entity existed independently of its identification as such, but its definition as Gothic was determined by a debate to which it was both marginal and essential: that of the future direction of architecture. The origin of the term 'Gothic' has been investigated by E. S. de Beer and shown to derive from the story of the Goths who invaded Rome and brought an end to the world of Antiquity.[4] This account became commonplace within the genre of art-historical writings emanating from Italy in the 15th and 16th centuries. At that time the *'maniera de' Goti'* referred to a manner of building which was still current, as one of the alternative terms, 'Modern', suggests. Both expressions related to the Renaissance view of history, which saw the recent past as a middle age, intervening, or blocking the way, between Antiquity and a desired future. De Beer's evaluation of many of the early uses of the term 'Gothic' as 'historical', rather than condemnatory, cannot evade the reality that for those who coined it, the purpose of writing was to celebrate those working in the new style and the very identification of a middle age was inherently damning, as was the use of the word 'Gothic' to describe its buildings. To be 'historical', therefore, was not to be neutral. We need also to be aware that 'Gothic' was never used as a noun defining an architectural style during the period under discussion – indeed, there was no general concept of a period style. The word 'Gothic' was always used adjectivally and often meant barbarous, rather as the word 'medieval' is used in present-day common parlance.[5] Its specific association with architecture is largely a 19th-century phenomenon.

Knowledge of the debates which defined Gothic appears to have been current in literary circles in England from the late 16th century, but it is clear that medieval architecture was by then already possessed of particular qualities. Evidence for some awareness of the Gothic legend is found in *Titus Andronicus,* the plot of which is based on the Gothic invasion of Rome. At the start of Act Five, a troop strays from the army of Goths outside Rome 'To gaze upon a ruinous Monastery'. The reference to a monastery is telling. In terms of the Italian origin of the story, had there been such a thing as a pensive Goth, he might have been expected to go out to gaze upon a desecrated temple or other Roman monument. The perceived crime of the Goths had been to extinguish the world of Antiquity, not Christianity. To an English audience, however, there was evidently truth in the idea that one might want to visit a ruined abbey. A famous quotation from *The Duchess of Malfi* reinforces this point when, in the echoing remnants of an ancient abbey, Antonio says to Delio,

> I doe love these auncient ruynes
> We never tread upon them, but we set
> Our foote upon some reverend History.[6]

Once dissolved by Henry VIII, English abbeys which were not converted to other uses served no functional purpose other than as stone quarries. Yet it is evident that they continued to be visited and were thus viewed in ways that transcended their original purposes. As Margaret Aston has shown, in England the so-called 'Renaissance view of the past' was shaped as much by religious changes as by a new attitude to the Classical inheritance.[7] This new attitude both shaped and was shaped by new attitudes to travel. In contrast to the Middle Ages, when most travel for which we have evidence had a functional purpose (notably pilgrimage), early modern travel could be undertaken for its own sake. Ruins were visited, as were unruined buildings, such as churches and castles, whose original functions remained intact. The majority of articulated responses to medieval architecture fall within the linked genres of topography and travel writing. Although, as we shall see, this is the context of the first English use of the term 'Gothic', its negative overtones are largely irrelevant to topographical descriptions. One of the main aims of topographical study was to develop local pride and it would therefore have been inappropriate to condemn what were, in most places, the majority of buildings discussed. This is yet more true of monographs on individual buildings: if the building were worthless, the book would also have little value. England already possessed means of describing medieval buildings which assigned them merits entirely independent of Classical values. When visitors went to see a medieval building, they did not do so with an entirely open mind. Attitudes and appropriate reactions were already available and, it seems, few were inclined to break free from a preconditioned response.

The class of sightseer most likely to record his or her experience of a cathedral or great house would usually have been taken round by a local guide, normally a verger employed by the Chapter or a servant of the owner of the property. The income of the guide would in part have depended on charges to visitors. Such custodians doubtless existed to guide pilgrims in the Middle Ages and oral traditions about buildings were already strong, eventually finding their way into published guidebooks, the printed equivalent of the personal escort. Because of its extremely commercial nature, this genre of literature was extraordinarily conservative and probably varied little from its medieval origins. Legends, elements of description and even long-destroyed architectural features were perpetuated in print and duly shaped the reaction of the visitor. The developing genre of travel literature catered both for those travelling, or planning to do so, and those whose journeying was limited to the pages of a book. Pocket guides which could be consulted *en route* contained the sorts of useful information required by the tourist and were produced at various levels of detail, from country-wide coverage to the *vade mecum* for a single town or monument. For the armchair traveller, published travel journals, such as Defoe's, provided the edification of travel, without its discomforts.

Many elements of what might be termed the topographical response seem to have been transmitted wholesale from the Middle Ages. The very words and categories of admiration are identical. Take, for example, Sampson Erdeswick (died *c.*1603) on Lichfield Cathedral:

In the close there is a goodly cathedral church, if I should say one of the fairest and best repaired in England …, I think I should speak no otherwise than the truth, and wherein also be a great number of very fair monuments of the bishops and other clergymen, besides divers others of the noblemen …

There are also, outwardly, builded, three pyramids or steeples, of a good, convenient, and seemly height, all very well wrought with free stone, especially the two gemels that stand westward, very well cut and curiously wrought. The which west part is, at the end also, exceedingly finely cut, and cunningly set forth with a great number of tabernacles; and in the same, the images or pictures of the prophets, apostles, kings of Judah, and divers other kings of this land, so well embossed, and so lively cut, that it is a great pleasure for any man, that takes delight in rarities, to behold them.[8]

Erdeswick's emphases may be found in innumerable medieval descriptions of buildings.[9] Likewise, his interest in ashlar is shared with John Leland some 50 years earlier. By the 17th century, Robert Plot structured the chapters on the arts in his natural histories to categorise buildings as examples of the art of working stone.[10] The vocabulary too is shared with both earlier and later writers; words like 'cunning' and 'embossed' are both frequent in medieval architectural discourse, whilst Celia Fiennes used almost the same words in 1697 when she described the tombs in St Mary's, Warwick as 'cut very finely' and 'curiously wrought'.[11] Here 'curiously' probably means skilfully, though curious could also mean singular.[12] The limitations of contemporary aesthetic vocabulary did not begin to be overcome until the 18th century and it is often difficult to understand exactly what was deemed admirable about particular edifices. It is clear that medieval buildings could be accorded admirable qualities which bore no relationship to the aesthetic norms of Classicism. On the other hand, these were also the very features which were condemned by those who sought to create and articulate a standard of polite taste. For Addison, the Gothic (though not medieval buildings *per se*) was characterised by its artificiality and superfluous ornamentation.[13]

The aesthetics of Lichfield Cathedral, however, were not central to Erdeswick's account. More important is his characterisation of the building as a 'rarity'. The identification of medieval relics as rarities or curiosities meant that their perusal could be profitable, even though they did not fall within contemporary canons of taste. Occasionally, parts of medieval buildings literally formed part of a cabinet of curiosities, as, for example, sculptures from York Minster in the museum of Ralph Thoresby at Leeds or the statues removed from the west front of Lichfield which became exhibits in Mr Greene's museum in the same city.[14] But for the responsive traveller, tourism turned every object encountered into a potential curiosity, which could broaden the mind and encourage local or national pride. If undertaken in the right spirit and by those able to profit from it, travel was felt to be inherently beneficial and the objects encountered partook of that value.

Rarities were thus defined by their benefit to the viewer. Catalogues of cabinets of curiosities made little effort to understand their contents in terms of their original context. What mattered was their present arrangement and meaning for the owner and visitor. It is evident that many collections contained items whose original meaning was specifically Catholic (for example, Greene's museum had numbers of crucifixes, rosaries and models of a Franciscan friar and a nun), yet in the context of the whole, these objects were evidently not problematic for a Protestant public. Returning again to Erdeswick's account, it seems that it is in this light that the statuary on the Lichfield west front is described. It is noticeable that although he recognised certain aspects of the iconography, Erdeswick either ignored or failed to recognise any Marian imagery. In fact, his interpretation is notably monarchical. His description was therefore not one which would have been challenging for mainstream Protestantism.

Evidently Erdeswick was not historicising Lichfield Cathedral as a monument to medieval Christianity. Both as a modern church and as a rarity, it had inherent moral value, which did not depend on its original meaning. For those who thought about the matter at all, any attempt to understand a church building historically would have been potentially problematic. Antiquarian authors were often (and sometimes rightly) suspected of harbouring Catholic sympathies. In the Middle Ages, churches were erected as both powerful symbols and spatial expressions of beliefs and practices which the more radical religious policies of the 16th century aimed to eradicate. Through iconoclasm, reformers attempted to restore to the simple state of the early Church ecclesiastical buildings which had never actually existed in that purified state, having been erected to provide the setting for the very trappings of 'popery' which were being stripped away. It may be assumed that such buildings continued to be recognised as a certain functional type based on their form. The word 'church' would probably have conjured up the familiar image of a medieval church, with characteristic features such as a tower, hall-like body and possibly even pointed-headed windows. Yet the 'Laudian' reformers, who apparently looked to medieval buildings for appropriate ecclesiological forms, did not usually do so in stylistic terms.[15]

Although in the Middle Ages, the temporal had never been absent from church buildings, the removal of much of the spiritual may have rendered the former more potent. Moreover, it became a matter of deliberate policy to place signs of secular power in the positions formerly held by the most significant religious exemplars; for example, the rood was replaced by the royal coat of arms. Tombs, protected from iconoclasm by royal decree, provided the most significant continuity between medieval and contemporary imagery and chantry chapels, already associated with burials, became nothing but mausolea once their altars were removed. Others remained private chapels, whilst fixed pews, belonging to particular families, proliferated. It is perhaps therefore not surprising that most descriptions of parish churches record only the heraldry of tombs and glass or, at most, the size of the building. To the contemporary mind, these were the most significant elements.

Yet, of course, interest in tombs also represents a

continuity from the Middle Ages. One of the most detailed medieval descriptions of an English building, Gervase's account of Canterbury Cathedral, had as its primary aim the location of the various tombs and shrines.[16] William Worcestre and Leland were extremely interested in who was buried where and this was obviously crucial to the work of medieval heralds, whose continuing concerns were to shape much early topographical and antiquarian endeavour. The first cathedral guidebook, Camden's 1600 account of Westminster Abbey, was largely an enumeration of the tombs, and this format proved very persistent. It was an interest shared by Continental viewers. Examination of the depictions of church interiors by Dutch 17th-century artists reveals that many contain figures studying graves, even apparently using guidebooks to do so.

Interest in funerary monuments appealed to a number of sensibilities. As monuments to great men, tombs served a moralising function and one in which buildings could be made to share. Descriptions of churches in topographical accounts focused in particular on who was responsible for erecting each portion. In part this reflects the textual sources used by the antiquarians, for medieval chronicles were careful to list works undertaken by bishops, abbots and lay patrons. Such information continued to be quoted, however, because it appealed to the persistent belief that architectural patronage was a work of piety and social utility and that celebrating past patrons would be an inspiration to potential benefactors in the present.

In addition, tombs provided a general *memento mori*, which again was deemed a worthy emotion. Weever's *Funerall Monuments* of 1631 aimed in part to stimulate such reverie and suggested also that buildings could evoke an analogous response:

> We desire likewise to behold the mournfull ruines of other religious houses, although their goodly faire structures bee altogether destroyed, their tombs battered downe, and the bodies of their dead cast out of their coffins; for that, that the very earth which did sometimes cover the corps of the defunct, puts vs in minde of our

mortalitie, and consequently brings vs to unfained repentence.[17]

Ruins, more than complete buildings, were deemed conducive to meditation on the transitory nature of earthly glory. In ruined state, a building represented both its own passing and that of its founders and thus corresponded to a tomb. Contemporaries were aware that ruins were equally, or even more, open to interpretative readings than complete buildings: as Aubrey wrote, 'the eie and mind is no lesse affected with these stately ruines than they would have been when standing and entire. They breed in generous mindes a kind of pittie; and sett the thoughts a-worke to make out their magnificence as they were when in perfection'.[18]

Meditation on the emptiness of worldly achievement has been a commonplace throughout history.[19] During the period under discussion, it was both cause and symptom of melancholia, defined as a disease affecting both the mental and the physical states. Whilst Burton advocated the study of antiquities as a cure for melancholy,[20] it was also a commonplace that ruins could provoke it. For example, at Eynsham in 1657, Anthony Wood 'was there wonderfuly strucken with a veneration of the stately, yet much lamented, ruins of the abbey there, built before the Norman Conquest ... He spent some time with a melancholy delight in taking a prospect of the ruins of that place ... The place hath yet some ruins to shew, and to instruct the pensive beholder with an exemplary frailty'.[21] This statement suggests that the ruins had an inherent meaning; Wood did not impose associations through his own imagination but was 'strucken' and thereby received instruction.

Although deemed a disease, melancholy seems to have been a state actively sought by Wood: for him it was 'delightful' and marked him out as a 'pensive beholder', able to benefit from the lessons the ruins offered. In the 1742 version of Defoe's travels, the editor noted that the scene of the ruins at Roche (Yorkshire) 'demands a serious Reverence from the Beholder, and inspires a contemplative Melancholy, oftentimes pleasing as well as proper to indulge'.[22] Melancholia was a mental and physical state which gave distinction to the sufferer. It was the condition of the lover (the cause of love-sickness) and the scholar. And increasingly during the 18th century, visitors came to ruins deliberately to demonstrate their own capacity for heightened sensibilities.

But here we run chronologically ahead of ourselves. If the motif of the ruin representing the triumph of Time over human endeavour has been a constant, nevertheless, from the 16th century, English ruins bore specific interpretations which are not a mere transference either from this eternal theme or from the Renaissance interest in the ruins of Antiquity. For those who welcomed the new religious order, the ruined state of the dissolved monasteries provided them with an appropriate set of symbols. Writing of the sadly desolate Canterbury in his *Perambulation of Kent* (1576), Lambarde praised God, 'that hath thus mercifully in our age deliuered us, disclosed Satan, unmasked these Idoles, disolued these Synagogues, and raced to the grounde all Monumentes of building, erected to superstition and ungodlinesse'.[23] For Lambarde, meaning here seems to be inherent and to derive from original purpose. From representing the power of the Church in England, monastic buildings now spoke of the overthrow of the Church of Rome. Echoes of this reading proved long-lasting; similar sentiments are still to be found in the 18th century and suggests that many who visited ruins did so without sympathy.

Lambarde, who supported the existing *status quo*, saw the downfall of the monasteries in positive terms but for others it was less welcome. Giacomo Soranzo, the Venetian (and, naturally, Roman Catholic) ambassador to England in 1554 reported on the city of London that it was much disfigured by ruins of churches and monasteries and blamed the Dissolution for food shortages.[24] Twenty-seven years later his successor, Daniele Barbaro, related that 'nothing is so mischievous as the destruction of the Abbacies, which maintained a great part of the population, were a refuge for the poor, a convenience for travellers, and profitable for the Sovereign in time of war'.[25] This information was presumably provided by English Catholic sympathisers, and throughout the 17th century conventual ruins continued to provoke similar readings by both Catholics and conservatives.

For Wood, just such a traditionalist, the ruins of Eynsham were rich in political resonance: the abbey was a royal foundation of the Saxon era. It was therefore a emblem of England's primitive (monarchical) constitution which, during the Commonwealth, was 'much lamented'. The instruction offered to the viewer by the ruin's 'exemplary frailty' suggests not just that the works of mankind in general were fragile, but something more personal. For those whose world-view had been shaken by the Civil War and the overthrow of the political order they had supported, ruins represented a very present threat to stability, a threat which was for some realised once again in both the 'Glorious Revolution' and the Hanoverian succession.

Secular ruins were also resonant with meaning. The motif of the ruin of an important dwelling representing the fall of its inhabitants had long been current but during the 16th century it may have seemed particularly relevant. Leland recorded over 170 castles which may be interpreted as being either dilapidated or entirely ruined, though whether through unrepaired damage during the civil wars of the 15th century or changes in living arrangements which rendered castles no longer convenient is not always clear.[26] After the Civil War of the 17th century, the importance of the castle as a military force was over and its symbolism was correspondingly transformed. To viewers mindful of an increased social mobility and of a higher rate of new building, old or ruined dwellings provided appropriate symbols of a passing era (whether this was to be lamented or celebrated).

As we have already seen, for the nostalgic, abbeys symbolised a departed source of charity. As early as the 16th century, the myth of Merrie England was already potent and old houses took on similar associations of munificence. In his diary, John Evelyn described such buildings as being modelled according to ancient hospitality. The metaphor also pervades country-house poetry, from Jonson's *To Penshurst* onwards.[27] Nevertheless, a building did not have to be specifically medieval to bear such associations; it was used for old houses of other periods by authors wishing to praise the owner of a property but unable to extol his or her taste in rebuilding it.

Interpretations of Medieval Architecture, *c.*1550–*c.*1750

The meanings of medieval architecture so far discussed were seen by contemporaries as inherent, though as with all emblems, recognition was dependent on the education of the observer. Its meanings, whether positive or negative were perceived to be exemplary and therefore educational. Medieval buildings therefore had a semiotic status of their own, which derived from their aesthetics according to medieval priorities or their functional purpose as church or castle etc. Their position was not dependent on their classification as medieval in period or Gothic in manner.

The first instance of the use of 'Gothic' as a classificatory term by an English speaker occurs in the diary of John Evelyn and it is likely that he learned the word whilst abroad. Earlier examples of its use in an English context are by a German who visited King's College Chapel in Cambridge in 1610 (and recorded his experience in French) and in Cotgrave's dictionary, already quoted (though this use is non-architectural). Evelyn's most famous use of the term occurs in the appendix to his translation of Fréart de Chambray's *Parallèle*. In describing the various branches of architecture, he stresses that he is intending to deal only with Greek and Roman architecture and not with 'a certain Fantastical and Licentious Manner of building, which we have since call'd *Modern* (or *Gothic* rather)' which he deems 'not worthy of the name of architecture'.[28] Despite claiming not to want to extend his discourse, Evelyn spends nearly two pages enumerating all the faults of Gothic, which are naturally all defined in terms of their departure from the Ancient ideal.

Until the 18th century, employment of the term 'Gothic' in the context of architectural theory was usually intended to stigmatise an existing manner of building and thereby to promote first the adoption and subsequently the use of what we should now term Classicism. The function of Gothic within this scheme is to define true Architecture (that is, the architecture of the Ancients) by identifying that which it is not. It would therefore be unlikely for statements made about Gothic in this situation to show any appreciation of the manner. Nevertheless, it is puzzling to consider why Evelyn was so vehement in his disapproval. Fréart's original text contains nothing of this nature: his disapproval was directed mainly against contemporary architects who departed from the rules of the antique masters (an alternative Other to Classicism). Even stranger is the fact that the digression occurs only in the second (1707) edition of the translation, which was first published in 1664.[29] The first edition contains only hints of Evelyn's anti-Gothic stance, and there the term is used to condemn incorrect usage of the orders, as Fréart had done, rather than buildings which may be identified as specifically medieval or Gothic in form.

Evelyn made a considerable number of other changes to the text published in 1707, which may go some way to explaining his diatribe. Following on from the new section on Gothic comes another addition, in which he points out the error in retaining existing parts of a building, or old foundations, or even carrying out repairs to dilapidated fabrics, rather than building entirely anew. He adds 'that since another *Edition* of this Piece is never likely to come under my hand again; I have taken the Liberty of *this* to speake my Thoughts the more freely; not without hope, that some may be Edified by it, and have cause to thank me for it'.[30] Other additions include a number of condemnations of workmen and their practices, especially contracting in the gross, and also references to treatises which had appeared since the first edition (d'Aviler, Blondel and Perrault).

Evelyn's revisions to his text were made in the context of an increase in architectural activity, in terms of both buildings and literature. The first edition came out soon after the Restoration; the second was written during the great expansion and post-Fire reconstruction of London and at a time when the return to political stability encouraged the numbers of the nobility to remodel or rebuild their houses. When writing of the 'great *Mistake*' of retaining existing elements, Evelyn may have been thinking of the debate over St Paul's Cathedral which followed the Great Fire. He and Sir Christopher Wren had rejected the suggestion of Sir Roger Pratt that the foundations of the crossing should be retained.[31] He might also have recalled his visit to Cassiobury (Hertfordshire), a house about which he wrote, ''tis pitty the house was not situated to more advantage; but it seemes it

Interpretations of Medieval Architecture, *c*.1550–*c*.1750

was built just where the old one was, & which I believe he onely meant to repair at first, which leads men into irremediable errors, & saves but little'.[32] Evelyn believed that architecture reflected society and, as he put it in 1664, 'It is from the *asymmetry* of our *Buildings*, want of *decorum* and proportion in our *Houses*, that the irregularity of our *humors* and *affections* may be shrewdly discerned'.[33] The retention of existing elements was a threat to the benefits offered by good architecture, both to the individual and the State. Although it is clear from his description that Evelyn had in mind the details of medieval buildings, the function of the passage is to reject the use of anything but Antique models, rather than specifically to condemn medieval architecture.[34]

In addition, it may not be too much to suggest that Evelyn could have been concerned about the future direction of architectural theory. It is clear from the 1707 edition that he had read both Blondel and Perrault and would therefore have been aware of the dispute between the Ancients and the Moderns. Fréart's text was deeply conservative and appealed to precedent, a course mainly followed by Evelyn. When writing of the propriety of using double columns on a single pedestal, he contrasted the views of Blondel (for whom it was unsanctioned by Antiquity and therefore wrong) and Perrault, who Evelyn described as being 'not so precisely oblig'd to Rules and Examples; but that in some Cases, they may safely be departed from for the better'.[35] Evelyn avoided having to choose between the two positions by noting that the feature does have Antique precedents and therefore may be used. Elsewhere, however, he echoed Perrault's position. Yet he might not have gone so far as his friend Wren, who, like Perrault, postulated two forms of beauty - natural and customary.[36] Whilst neither Perrault nor Wren used their belief in customary beauty to argue that there might be elements in Gothic worthy of emulation, Evelyn could perhaps have recognised the threat to Vitruvian Classicism that their theories implied. And it was certainly not long before theorists did indeed begin to suggest that modern architects could learn from medieval architecture. That the debate was between Ancients and Moderns meant that Gothic ('Modern') architecture was by definition available as a potential model. And by the early 18th century, in the works of the Perrault-inspired authors Michel de Frémin and the Abbé de Cordemoy, a theoretical basis was laid for the appreciation of Gothic.[37] Yet although Batty Langley and William Halfpenny were to publish pattern books for buildings in the 'Gothick taste', no theoretical treatise emerged to deal with the rules of building in the style until Sir James Hall (1798).[38]

Architectural theory accorded Gothic a transgressive or oppositional status, which was to prove very fruitful of meanings. Already in 1602, the poet Samuel Daniel made inventive use of Italianate theory in his *Defence of Ryme*. Here, he supported English poetic traditions against those, specifically Thomas Campion, who proposed closer reliance on Latin models. Daniel cited the laws and constitutions of the post-Classical European nations as proof that the Goths had not completely destroyed learning (as in the model explanation) but had made their own intellectual contribution. He mentioned a number of medieval authors to prove that literacy had not entirely been extinguished and proposed that all ages contained some worthy aspects. As a final point, he wrote, 'Let vs go no further, but look vpon the wonderfull Architecture of this state of *England* and see whether they were deformed times, that could give it such a forme'.[39] Daniel's argument has persuasively been interpreted as a defence of native architectural traditions.[40] The same genre of treatises through which the Gothic story was transmitted also drew parallels between the revival of Antique forms in architecture and literature and Daniel may thus have been reversing the motif.[41] Nevertheless, the quotation should not necessarily be read as a vindication of the forms of Gothic architecture, for Daniel goes on to elaborate on his theme of the worth of medieval times:

> Where there is no one the least piller of Maiestie, but was set with the most profound iudgement and borne up with the iust conueniecie of Prince and people. No Court of Iustice, but laide by the Rule and Square of Nature, and the best of the best commonwealths that euer were in the world.

Interpretations of Medieval Architecture, *c.*1550–*c.*1750

Here the use of architectural elements is clearly alle-
gorical and refers not to medieval buildings as such but the
English constitution. A constitutional reading thus adds a further level to the arguments of the text in its entirety than
would a purely architectural one. Indeed, it is unclear to what
extent, before Inigo Jones and his circle, an English viewer
would have been able to draw distinctions between the
Gothic and Classical traditions in architecture which went
beyond theoretical terms learned from Continental treatises
(but not necessarily suited to interpreting English buildings)
or a simple recognition of old versus new.

The association of the word 'Gothic' with the English
constitution was extremely persistent. As befits something
unwritten, the constitution was defined as much by what it
was not, as by what it was. At a time when Classicism formed
the normal mode of building for all shades of political
opinion and the erection of new buildings was used to
symbolise authority, Gothic or old buildings could be used to
represent opposition to the governing power, either nega-
tively or positively. When Antique forms were used to express
legitimacy, Gothic could stand for chaos. When Classicism
was defined as foreign, illiberal, modern or grandiose, Gothic
could be seen as its converse. For example, in 1739, we find
an anonymous author in *Common Sense* writing,

> Methinks there was something respectable in those old
> hospitable *Gothick* Halls, hung round with Helmets,
> Breast-Plates, and Swords of our Ancestors; I entered
> them with a Constitutional Sort of Reverence, and
> look'd upon those Arms with Gratitude as the Terror of
> former Ministers, and the Check of Kings. Nay, I even
> imagin'd that I saw some of those good Swords, that had
> procur'd the Confirmation of *Magna Charta*, and hum-
> bled *Spencers* and *Gavestons*. And when I see these thrown
> by, to make way for some tawdry Gilding and Carving, I
> can't help considering such an Alteration as ominous
> even to our Constitution. Our old *Gothick* Constitution
> had a noble Strength and Simplicity in it, which was well
> enough represented by the bold Arches and solid Pillars
> of the edifices of those days.[42]

Samuel Kliger has provided a compendious account of the association between Gothic architecture and the Gothic constitution.[43] It is clear that the association was general – all medieval buildings could be associated with the original constitution, not merely those of pre-Conquest origin. It was not even necessary that the building be truly medieval: Horace Walpole wrote in a letter that the newly-built folly at Hagley exhibited the 'true Rust of the Barons' Wars'.[44] Kliger associated the metaphor with a single tradition of political discourse which he saw developing within Parliamentarianism in the early-to-mid 17th century and which became part of Whig ideology in the later 17th and 18th centuries. Yet although many 17th-century Parliamentarians admired what they interpreted as the Gothic constitution, few would have expressed any admiration for Gothic cathedrals. And Royalists, like Wood, could connect Gothic architecture and the primitive constitution in quite a different way.

Although anonymous, the 1739 passage is interpreted by Kliger as representing a Whig position.[45] Looking at the quotation in the context both of the article from which it comes and other pieces from *Common Sense* quoted in the *Gentleman's Magazine*, however, the picture becomes more complex. The article as a whole is a criticism of the modern fashion for spending vast sums of money on building and gardening. Such satire was commonplace in the early-to-mid 18th century.[46] Our author condemns such expenditure, in particular by those who can ill-afford it and are drawn into corruption to pay for it. He says it seldom demonstrates taste, which in any case is mutable, sacrifices convenience, and rarely displays magnificence, as few can carry their schemes to completion. Here he echoes Evelyn in condemning the addition of Venetian windows and Grecian porticos to old, decaying mansions. It is in this context that he suggests existing Gothic buildings should be retained. The piece then finishes with a moral tale, which describes a visit made to the country residence belonging to the neighbour of a friend. Much had been spent in making additions to his estate. The author was shown a temple and obelisk, erected the summer after the Excise Bill (1733); a splendid bed-chamber and ante-chamber, constructed after the Prince's affair in

Parliament (1737); and, the most splendid addition, the 'Convention room' (presumably named after the Convention of El Pardo). The owner of the house was a member of Parliament, who had spent much of his fortune in securing his election. The inference of corruption is evident and from the instances on which bribes seem to have been taken, it seems clear that he was no supporter of Walpole. The specific points of satire therefore suggest that the author is operating not from a Whig or Tory stance but expressing views characteristic of what historians have termed 'Country ideology'.[47] In the 1730s, this was voiced in particular by the 'Patriot' group, which transcended party lines.

Country ideology, which developed in the second half of the 17th and continued to be important into the 18th century, contained many strands. It was both pro-Parliament, seeking parliamentary scrutiny of the executive and demanding regular and frequent elections, and supportive of the landed classes, aiming to reduce both the number of placemen in Parliament and the influence of those who derived their status from office. Country ideology thus formed a discourse of opposition which was available to either Whigs or Tories who felt that their interests were not being represented by the government of the day. It is probable that the *Common Sense* passage, with its complaints of parliamentary corruption, implicit opposition to taxation, and allusions to specific Patriot triumphs, is drawn from this position. The bulk of articles reproduced in the *Gentleman's Magazine* in 1739 also reflect this tendency: they are supportive of the constitution, yet voice a widely-held belief that freedoms and liberties are being betrayed; they speak against parliamentary corruption, yet are afraid of the popular tendency to criticise politicians; they are supportive of the War of Jenkins' Ear, yet oppose the growth in state expenditure which war required.

Seeing Gothic as but one of the many metaphors employed to represent opposition in political discourse helps us to understand why it could be used both for its positive and its negative connotations by both Whigs and Tories. It was not, as Kliger suggested, that party politics conditioned taste in the arts, but that objects which we normally interpret in artistic terms could be used in other contexts to provide commonly-understood points of reference. To begin to interpret the status of Gothic or medieval buildings, we need to examine the function they played within the discourse. Their meaning may be defined as much by what they are not, as by what they are. We also need to make a distinction between Gothic buildings (which may or may not be medieval) and buildings which we know to be medieval but which earlier viewers may not have interpreted in period-specific terms. This does not, however, make it any easier for the modern scholar to identify what a Gothic building meant to its historical viewers. To understand responses, we are thrown back on identifying the interpretive stance of the speaker, just as we have to do to understand the motivation of a builder using a Gothic style. Both writing about medieval Gothic buildings and building new ones are creative acts, but ones which cannot be divorced from existing discourses. Texts and buildings co-exist; one does not lay the foundations for the other. What is clear, however, is that even before its appreciation in terms of the Sublime and the Picturesque, Gothic had a multiplicity of possible interpretations, each of which could be used to different ends.

Notes

1 The many works based around this premise include C. L. Eastlake, *A History of the Gothic Revival in England* (London, 1872); K. Clark, *The Gothic Revival. An Essay in the History of Taste* (London, 1928); W. D. Robson-Scott, *The Literary Background of the Gothic Revival in Germany* (Oxford, 1965); M. McCarthy, *The Origins of the Gothic Revival* (New Haven and London, 1987).

2 As has been done (in relation to ruins only) by M. Andrews, *The Search for the Picturesque* (Stanford, 1989), pp. 41–5, where he divides responses into the sentimental response, the antiquarian response, the aesthetic response and the moral response. Other works, cited below, concentrate on single categories.

3 For interpretive communities, see S. Fish, *Is there a Text in This Class? The Authority of Interpretive Communities* (Cambridge, Massachussetts and London, 1980).

4 E. S. de Beer, 'Gothic: Origin and Diffusion of the Term; the Idea of Style in Architecture', *Journal of the Warburg and Courtauld Institutes*, 11 (1948), pp. 143-62. The term 'Romanesque' was not

invented until the 19th century and for the purposes of this essay, the word 'Gothic' will be used to cover both styles.

5 See Cotgrave's 1611 French-English dictionary, the earliest use of the word in English. There the definition of Gothique is given as 'Gothlike; rude, cruell, barbarous'. R. Cotgrave, *A Dictionarie of the French and English Tongues* (London, 1611); reprinted with introduction by W. S. Woodes (New York, 1950). It is unclear from what source Cotgrave learned the term.

6 J. Webster, *The Duchess of Malfi*, Act 5, Scene 3.

7 M. Aston, 'English Ruins and English History: the Dissolution and the Sense of the Past', *Journal of the Warburg and Courtauld Institutes*, 36 (1973), pp. 231-55.

8 S. Erdeswick, *A Survey of Staffordshire*, edited by T. Harwood (London, 1820), p. 210.

9 For example, 'wele and workmanly wrought' is a constant refrain in the contracts for King's College Chapel, Cambridge (1512-13): L. F. Salzman, *Building in England down to 1540* (Oxford, 1952), pp. 564-70.

10 R. Plot, *The Natural History of Oxfordshire, being an Essay towards the Natural History of England* (Oxford, 1677) and *The Natural History of Staffordshire* (Oxford, 1686). The chapters on the arts form chapter nine of both books. Plot seems to have made no value judgement between medieval and modern buildings as examples of this art.

11 *The Journeys of Celia Fiennes*, edited by C. Morris (London, 1949), p. 115.

12 'Curious' and 'curiosities' could also be used in disparaging terms, even in the Middle Ages. See, for example, the contract for the Divinity Schools, Oxford (1439-40) or the preliminary specification for Eton College (1447-8): Salzman, op. cit. [note 9], pp. 513-14 and 522-6.

13 *The Spectator*, 63 (May 12, 1711) describes a dream on True and False wit, in which the Region of False Wit includes a Temple of Dullness described as a 'Monstrous Fabrick built after the Gothick manner and covered with Innumerable Devices in that barbarous kind of Sculpture', *The Spectator*, edited by D. F. Bond (Oxford, 1965), volume 1, p. 271. It should be stressed, however, that the function of Addison's metaphors was not architectural but literary. In his previous article, he had used 'Gothick' with no architectural referent, to condemn the taste of most English poets and readers (ibid., p. 269), as the previous year in *The Tatler* he used the word to contrast a laboured literary style with the simple manner of the Ancients: *The Tatler*, no. 163 (April 25, 1710), edited by D. F. Bond (Oxford, 1987), volume 2, p. 407. Similarly Steele in the same

periodical (no. 177, May 27, 1710) used the superfluity of Gothic as a metaphor to condemn eulogistic book dedications: ibid., p. 465.

14 R. Thoresby, *Ducatus Leodiensis* (London, 1715), p. 487 and p. 567; *A Descriptive Catalogue of the Rarities, in Mr. Greene's Museum at Lichfield* (Lichfield, 1773), p. 8.

15 Most of the new work by this group which could be interpreted as programmatic is not Gothic in style. It is also possible that apparently medieval arrangements were inspired by contemporary Lutheran churches in Germany and especially Scandinavia, where the Reformation had never taken a Calvinist turn and so had not swept away existing features, including medieval fittings and imagery.

16 Gervase's aim in writing was apparently to convince his readers than none of the important shrines and tombs had been lost in the great fire but were now housed in a more appropriate setting: *The Chronicle of the Reigns of Stephen, Henry II, and Richard I by Gervase, the Monk of Canterbury*, edited by W. Stubbs (Rolls Series, 1879), pp. 3-16 and 25-6.

17 J. Weever, *Ancient Funerall Monuments* (London, 1631), p. 41.

18 *Wiltshire. The Topographical Collections of John Aubrey*, edited by J. E. Jackson (Devizes, 1862), p. 4.

19 R. Macaulay, *Pleasure of Ruins* (London, 1953).

20 R. Burton, *The Anatomy of Melancholy*, edited by N. K. Kiessing, T. C. Faulkner and R. L. Blair, with commentary by J. B. Bamborough and M. Dodsworth (Oxford, 1989-2000), volume 2, p. 76 advocated the study of pictures of great buildings of Antiquity (including buildings now ruined or demolished, which might normally be expected to be a cause of melancholy) and on pp. 84-95 advocates study, including contemplation, of rarities, such as 'old reliques' (which are distinguished from Roman antiquities).

21 A. Clark, *The Life and Times of Anthony Wood, Antiquary of Oxford, 1632-1695, Described by Himself* (Oxford Historical Society, 1891), volume 1, p. 228.

22 D. Defoe, *A Tour Thro' the Whole Island of Great Britain*, 4 volumes (third edition, London, 1742), volume 3, p. 98.

23 W. Lambarde, *A Perambulation of Kent* (London, 1576), p. 236.

24 *Calendar State Papers, Venetian*, 5 (1534-54), (London, 1873), no. 934, p. 543.

25 Ibid., no. 703, p. 347.

26 M. W. Thompson, *The Decline of the Castle* (Cambridge, 1989), pp. 171-8.

27 R. A. Aubin, *Topographical Poetry in XVIII-century England* (New York 1936); A. Fowler, *The Country House Poem* (Edinburgh, 1994).

28 J. Evelyn, 'Account of Architects and Architecture', appendix to his translation of *Parallèle de l'architecture antique et de la moderne* by Roland de Fréart (London, 1707), p. 8.

29 From the evidence of the dedication, the second edition was written in 1696/7. Unfortunately, Evelyn's diary for this period does not survive.

30 Ibid., p. 13.

31 *The Diary of John Evelyn*, edited by E. S. de Beer (Oxford, 1955), volume 3, pp. 448-9.

32 Ibid., volume 4, p. 200.

33 J. Evelyn, dedicatory epistle to Sir John Denham in his translation of Parallèle de l'architecture antique et de la-moderne by Roland de Fréart (London, 1664).

34 A contrast between Evelyn's private and public statements on architecture has therefore been suggested by K. Downes, 'John Evelyn and Architecture: a first Inquiry', in *Concerning Architecture. Essays on Architectural Writers and Writing Presented to Nikolaus Pevsner*, edited by J. Summerson (London, 1968), p. 35.

35 J. Evelyn, op. cit. [note 28], p. 49.

36 L. M. Soo, *Wren's "Tracts" on Architecture and other Writings* (Cambridge, 2000), pp. 119-52.

37 For the French treatises, see H.-W. Kruft, *A History of Architectural Theory from Vitruvius to the Present* (London and New York, 1994), pp. 139-42; J. McQuillan, 'From Blondel to Blondel: on the Decline of the Vitruvian Treatise', in V. Hart with P. Hicks (editors), *Paper Palaces. The Rise of the Renaisannce Architectural Treatise* (New Haven and London, 1998), pp. 338-57, esp. pp. 351-2 and R. D. Middleton, 'The Abbé de Cordemoy and the Graeco-Gothic Ideal: a prelude to Romantic Classicism', *Journal of the Warburg and Courtauld Institutes*, 25 (1962), pp. 278-320 and 26 (1963), pp. 90-123.

38 Sir J. Hall, 'Essay on the Origin and Principles of Gothic Architecture', in *Transactions of the Royal Society of Edinburgh*, 4 (1798), papers of the literary class pp. 1-27.

39 S. Daniel, *Poems and a Defence of Ryme*, edited by A. Colby Sprague (Cambridge, Mass., 1930), pp. 145-6, lines 583-91.

40 C. Anderson, 'Learning to Read Architecture in the English Renaissance', in Lucy Gent (editor), *Albion's Classicism. The Visual Arts in Britain, 1550-1660, Studies in British Art, 2* (New Haven and London, 1995), p. 284.

41 This comparison is made by Alberti, Filarete and Serlio, as well as by the literary theorist Pietro Bembo. See P. Davies and D. Hemsoll, 'Sanmicheli's Architecture and Literary Theory', in G. Clarke and P. Crossley (editors), *Architecture and Language.*

Constructing Identity in European Architecture c.1000-c.1650 (Cambridge, 2000), pp. 102-17.

42 Reprinted in *The Gentleman's Magazine*, 9 (1739), p. 641.

43 S. Kliger, *The Goths in England* (Cambrdige, Massachussetts, 1952).

44 Letter from Walpole to Bentley, September 1753, in W. S. Lewis, A. D. Wallace and R. A. Smith (editors), *The Correspondence of Horace Walpole*, volume 35 (New Haven and London, 1973), p. 148.

45 Kliger, op. cit. [note 43], pp. 4-5 and p. 28.

46 B. Sprague Allen, *Tides in English Taste (1619-1800). A Background for the Study of Literature*, (Cambridge, Massachussetts, 1937), volume 1, pp. 97-113.

47 D. Hayton, 'The "Country" Interest and the Party System, 1689-c.1720', in *Party and Management in Parliament, 1660-1784*, edited by C. Jones (Leicester, 1984), pp. 37-85.

2

The Historiography of
'Elizabethan Gothic'

The Historiography of 'Elizabethan Gothic'

The Historiography of 'Elizabethan Gothic'

Maurice Howard

THE DESCRIPTIVE term 'Elizabethan Gothic' is used here courtesy of two precedents from very different moments in the past critical evaluation of styles and of style labels. In the 19th century, when so many of our basic assumptions about the characteristics of stylistic difference were argued over and set down with profuse illustration, the terms 'Elizabethan' and 'Gothic' were largely kept separate. They were joined at the hip, however, on one famous occasion, when, following the fire of 1834, the competition for the new Houses of Parliament called for designs of either Elizabethan or Gothic, both felt to represent something of the English past (and it was emphatically an English, rather than British, set of guidelines proposed).[1] It is possible that an outcome might have been entertained that consisted of a compromise between the two. They were yoked together here in a nationalist cause because they were both felt to be emphatically non-Classical, Classicism being given a restructured identity that allied it to foreign ways of building. The other precedent comes from a century and a quarter later, with the publication in 1963 of Mark Girouard's article 'Elizabethan Architecture and the Gothic Tradition', a different juxtaposition of the two terms that enabled the author to explore the way late-16th-century architecture paid its respects to not just a distant but a quite recent past of sixty or seventy years earlier, from the time of the early Tudor kings.[2] This chapter will use the term 'Elizabethan Gothic' in a very particular way. It seeks to explore the differences between stylistic revivals that are deliberate and programmatic and those which use the past more loosely and unselfconsciously, to suggest a continuum with what has gone before. It will suggest that there were distinctive breaks or changes in the aims and processes of looking back.[3]

In the longer view of Gothic as a dynamic and creative source of inspiration, something else has to be tackled before

Opposite:
Great Hall, Burghley House, Northamptonshire (*Country Life Picture Library*).

Haddon Hall,
Derbyshire,
panelling, Long
Gallery (*Country
Life Picture Library*).

we go further. For many writers the issue has been less one
of Gothic Revival than one of 'Gothic Survival'. It is true
that we can find examples of features of Gothic style in
buildings of all kinds at all periods between the Reformation
and the early 19th century. It is certainly the case that for
generations of builders and craftsmen throughout the 16th
and into the 17th century, the practices of the Gothic past
remained dominant in their methods of proceeding. For a
long time after the style and technical procedures of
Perpendicular ceased to be evolving, in a period of only spo-
radic restoration, rather than new building, of churches in the
post-Reformation period, it nevertheless continued to cast a
long shadow over the practice of domestic architecture.
Perhaps one of the key examples of this is the planning and
drawing out of the vertical bay, at an early period between
piers or buttresses, then later increasingly between Classical
pilasters or half columns, in secular building. The width of the
bay was invariably always planned as if it needed to encompass the broad, four-centred arches of the Perpendicular style.
It took a long time, even where Classical mouldings, a symmetry of the number and placing of window openings, and

indeed the Classical orders themselves, were all in place – as, say, at Longleat in the 1570s – for craftsmen to modify what they practised as customary. The skills and inclination to follow Classical principles in the relationship of window height to width and the ratio of window space to wall in the arrangement of the bay, as explained and illustrated with greatest influence in the books of Serlio, took a long time to evolve.

The reluctance to conceive the bay as being of different proportions – or it may have been the deliberate decision not to change old ways – provided a particularly interesting evolution in the history of wood panelling for interiors. In panelling, the Classical module was not necessarily the starting-point for the introduction of Classical ornament. The display of creative skills remained paramount. High bases served as plinths to squat pilasters and the anxiety to add pattern in every conceivable space pulled the design away from Classical proportion and order towards the articulation of panelling that was more like a complex pictorial field than an affirmation of the internal proportions of the room. Framing inlaid illusion or heraldry was often more important than repeating the module. The panelling of about 1600 in the gallery at Haddon Hall, for example, is better understood alongside the screen of a late medieval chantry chapel than against the rhythm of the facade of a 16th-century Florentine palazzo.[4] Hence the very different panelling of the 'Haynes Grange' Room, in the Victoria and Albert Museum, with its almost correct Serlian proportions and its absence of ornament, has proved hard to date across a range from the 1550s to the 1620s, although a possible *terminus post quem* has recently been suggested from the print source for the ornament of the fireplace. When and why, in this particular instance, was a more strictly Serlian set of principles adopted and how did the joiners acquire their new skills?[5]

This continuity of Gothic practice is perhaps most usefully called 'Tudor Gothic' or even 'Tudor and Jacobean Gothic'. Chris Brooks's *The Gothic Revival* has a useful checklist of the key features of the holding-on to past practice: string courses or labels over shallow arched doors and windows, open timbered roofs, and pointed windows, cusped and traceried for chapels.[6] The period covered by 'Elizabethan Gothic', as employed in the present paper, uses all these forms but the term itself is a useful descriptor of a different kind. Turning our backs on the concept of an unbroken and uncritical 'Gothic Survival' and taking a cue from Girouard's 1963 article, it is apparent that Gothic Revival comes in different shapes at different times and for different purposes. 'Elizabethan Gothic' is useful therefore for that attitude of the late 16th and early 17th centuries that looked to the past not to copy with any exactitude past styles and ornament, but more to evoke a mythical, invented version of the medieval past. This was meant to express national unity at a time of internal religious upheaval and external threat, and social respectability to those classes who claimed the chief positions of power.

To return, however, in order to establish a history of definitions, to the 19th century, when styles were identified as necessarily separate and sequential. For the Victorians, defining the term 'Elizabethan' proved straightforward in terms of evidence, complex in terms of its allegiance to past or future. For 19th-century writers, the dominant style of the late 16th and early 17th centuries, commonly known as Elizabethan, was primarily defined in terms of ornament. Their disagreement, however, as to whether this ornament could be categorised as Gothic or Classical first suggested the sense that it was neither one nor the other. At its best and most inventive, Elizabethan style was necessarily at odds with the restraint of pure Classicism. It used the ornament of the Classical vocabulary very forcefully, inflating the scale of figurative and abstract motifs, using them inventively across genres of building and often rendering them with high colour for emphasis. In the eyes of C. J. Richardson, writing in 1837, Elizabethan was suitable only for lesser, smaller buildings, since he opposed the spirit of the Houses of Parliament competition by arguing that Classical remained correct for large public projects. He writes of the Elizabethan style's 'quaint gables, fantastic pinnacles and pendants; its intricate parapets and grotesque carvings' which 'connect themselves intimately with surrounding scenery and form a picture far more readily and agreeably than uniform symmetrical objects.'[7]

Richardson here sees 'Elizabethan' in terms of extravagant outline and profile; for other 19th-century writers it was a strong and wilful ornament but one necessarily expressed within . a Classical framework. J. B. Waring, writing for Owen Jones in *The Grammar of Ornament* (1856), is emphatic that this ornamental style, deriving principally by the late 16th century from Germany and the Netherlands rather than Italy, had abandoned the shapes and structures of Gothic and taken on Classical forms as its chosen framework. 'Unlike the earliest examples of the revival on the Continent', he writes, 'especially in France and Spain, these ornaments are not applied to Gothic forms; but the groundwork or architectural mass is essentially Italian in its nature (except in the case of windows): consisting of a rough application of the orders of architecture one over another, external walls with cornice and balustrade, and internal walls bounded with frieze and cornice, with flat or covered ceilings; even the gable ends, with their convex and concave outlines, so common in the style, were founded on the models of the early Renaissance school at Venice'.[8]   If Waring is correct, then this was a fundamental break with the early 16th century, when the first hints in England of Renaissance running-ornament are found in conventional Gothic mouldings, especially evident in an important handful of surviving chantry chapels before the Reformation, and certain church fittings, such as choir stalls.

In the later 20th century, a series of what proved to be highly-respected and authoritative texts explored a new conception of Elizabethan that was not so much a definable style but a hybrid of several others. This analysis could at one level simply operate by pointing to what might seem to the architectural purist some apparently startling juxtapositions between Classical and Gothic, demonstrating a deliberate clash of past and present. The true path of stylistic evolution was that one method or 'style' should inevitably follow another, avoiding confusion and conflation. In the entry passage through the gatehouse of Charlecote Park, Warwickshire, probably built during the 1550s, Pevsner, in *Buildings of England* (1966), noted what he saw as a stylistic contradiction in features that for him stood either side of an

inevitable stylistic progression: 'a rib vault with pendants (still), and to the l. and r. niches with shell apses (already)'.[9] Other writers, principally Eric Mercer, John Summerson and Mark Girouard, tended not to make implied judgments about the inappropriateness of such clashes of style but rather asked whether they were happening to good purpose.[10]

Examining the planning of buildings, these writers all noted the mix of past and present working at an intricate and subtle level; as Palladio's, Serlio's and Du Cerceau's plans inspired English buildings, they were adapted to particular English needs. The foreign treatises' carefully proportioned spaces were stretched and elongated, turning central open courtyards into traditional English great halls, devising extruded corner turrets not as series of symmetrical apartments but as convenient spaces for stairs, garderobes and secure tower chambers. The basic symmetry of the continental plan is preserved but adapted to incorporate new ideas alongside traditional domestic needs of the wealthy English building patron. These new understandings in the later 20th century of the ingenuity of the Elizabethan style emerged from a growing interest in the past half-century in using Elizabethan architecture as a measure of certain wider historical ideas than style; developments that were social, political and domestic. Deborah Howard has skilfully applied this choosing of aspects of style to demarcate particular social class amongst the buildings of 16th- and 17th-century Scotland.[11] Choice of style can be to do with individual taste, but it can also indicate a sense of belonging. Much recent writing has therefore stressed the fissures, the alternatives, the choices that patrons made. In this context, Timothy Mowl's *Elizabethan and Jacobean Style* (1993), which has a short polemical text and lavish illustrations, was a shot at restoring the paramountcy of style to the period in a way more akin to the approach of 19th-century writers.[12]

The situation is different in terms of definitions when we look back to the period itself when Gothic and Renaissance cohabited. For a variety of reasons it was important for European contemporaries of the Elizabethans, and especially continental theorists, to stress Gothic as different from their new allegiance to Classical principles. One line of argument condemned Gothic as an aberration. The chief responsibility for the castigation of Gothic as unlettered and chaotic has usually been laid at the door of Giorgio Vasari. He never used the term as an adjectival descriptor of a style, though he did write of '*la maniera de' Goti*', without implying criticism, for certain works of the 12th and 13th centuries. More frequently, he referred to '*lavoro tedesco*' or the '*maniera tedesca*' as a way of pinning the anti-Classical style on to influences from outside Italy, which he refers to ubiquitously as 'German', responsible for late-medieval building campaigns in the Gothic style at certain great churches. But he takes it further than this. When Italian artists or architects fall into error even with their command of the Classical, they can be accused of slipping into the bad habits of this alien and undisciplined mode. In comparison with the earlier solutions of Bramante and Raphael and the later resolution of Michelangelo, the model of St Peter's, Rome, left by Antonio da Sangallo the Younger at his death in 1546 is described as having 'too many rows of columns one above another, and that with all its projections, spires and subdivisions of members it derived more from the German manner than from either the sound method of the ancient world or the graceful and lovely style followed by modern artists.'[13] What Vasari signals here is the sense that the style foreign to the Classicism of Italy is too detailed and finicky to demonstrate a grasp of the overall principles of design.

In England, it is predictably only in the 17th century, among the court cognoscenti, the circle of Inigo Jones and the Earl of Arundel, that the word 'Gothic' is first used consistently as a derogatory term, though initially 'Goths' were destroyers of a rich, ancient past. The speech delivered by the Lady of the Lake, written by Ben Jonson for the masque *Prince Henry's Barriers*, presented in January 1610, includes a paean of praise for the lost House of Chivalry:

> When every stone was laid by virtuous hands
> And standing so (O that it yet not stands!)
> More truth of architecture there was blazed
> Than lived in all the ignorant Goths have razed.[14]

A sense of grudging acknowledgment of painstaking effort alongside mistaken choice of style emerges from Arundel's description of Milan Cathedral in his instructions to John Evelyn of 1646:

> The Domo the prime church is of an infinite charge and will hardly ever be finished, but hath misfortune to be done on an ill designe of ye Gothick architecture ... it's worth one's paines going up to the top of ye church to see the infinite charge of adorning with carvings and other figures.'[15]

Alongside this condemnatory judgment, however, there grew a different sense of Gothic as certainly from a distant time and inappropriate for contemporary building, but belonging to a past that is nevertheless worthy of admiration. Sebastiano Serlio's term for Gothic is '*opera moderna*', that is to say the style of recent times that now has given way to the Classical revival. Its very difference enables an experienced and well-trained eye, such as John Evelyn's, to distinguish styles and note where awkward juxtapositions of style resulted in the hybrid form. Evelyn appears to have tuned his response to Gothic according to the polemics of his different genres of writing. When he translates and edits the texts of other writers or suggests a theoretical approach to building, he puts Gothic to the sword. When, however, he travels, observes and records buildings he has seen, he is sympathetic, even moved. As an appendix to the second, 1707 edition of his translation of Fréart's *Parallèle*, Evelyn is condemnatory of this 'Fantastical and Licentious manner of Building, which we have since call'd Modern (or Gothic rather)'.[16] His earlier diary entries, however, strike a different note. Audley End in 1654 is 'a mixt fabric twixt antique and modern' and in 1670 'indeed a cheerful piece of Gotic-building, or rather antico-moderno, but placed in an obscure bottom'. At Haarlem in 1641, the town is described as 'very delicat ... and hath one of the fairest churches of the Gothique design I had ever seen'.[17]

Out of this distinction between 'antique' and 'modern' came the first statements of a theory of appropriateness and one of national pride that were to form distinct parts of the debate between styles thereafter. Appropriateness gave Gothic a place, but a lowly one, in the hierarchy of styles. In his celebrated juxtaposition of comic and tragic scenes in Book II, first published in 1541, Serlio outlined the built environment of his townscape, noting the necessary domestic and service buildings, distinct from the great and public structures: 'this first shall be comicall, whereas the houses must be right for citizens, but specially there must not want a brawthell or a bawdy house, and great Inne, and a church; such things are of necessitie to be therein'.[18] This translation of Serlio's text comes from the 1611 Robert Peake edition, the first in the English language, in which the woodcuts were taken from the edition of Serlio first published in Antwerp in the 1540s:

the buildings for the ordinary citizens to live in and take their bodily pleasures have pointed arches over the windows. These images would already have been well-known to those 16th-century English patrons versed in architectural theory and practice, since earlier, foreign editions of Serlio were commonly found in their libraries.[19]

The national dimension to this distinction of the 'modern' Gothic, a style of the recent past, from the timeless style of the Classical world, by now in the 16th century in the full swing of revival, is most clearly articulated by Philibert de l'Orme's *Architecture* (1548). The lowliness of Gothic's stylistic status here gives way to admiration for its technical achievement. Here, in three chapters on Gothic in Book Four, De l'Orme describes ribbed vaults, which he says workmen describe as '*à la mode Françoise*'.[20] He admires the technical method of making these vaults, but says that their solution to vaulting is not now followed; spherical vaults rather are praised for their reliability and their comparative cheapness. This sets up therefore, for those looking to the national past for example and precedent, a home-grown alternative to the dominance of Classicism. For De l'Orme this technical facility is worthy of admiration, but as a viable style it is now foreclosed; for others, the very instance of national Gothic 'solutions' would provide a rallying point not in terms of debating the merits of stylistic integrity as such, but as flags of convenience when the political situation demanded different values in architecture to those employed by rulers and other classes of people currently in power.

Castigation, separateness, and an honourable past were all ways, therefore, of creating difference and ultimately of pointing to choice. It would be wrong to transfer back to the 16th and 17th centuries that 19th-century confidence, referred to at the start of this article in connection with the Houses of Parliament competition, about the exact correspondence of any given style with a notion of national identity. This is not least because notions of national identity are constantly shifting, as indeed are English attitudes to whatever is seen in opposition to those ideas from Italian or French sources. There is no question that from the time of the earliest laments about the Dissolution of the monasteries from the mid-16th century onwards, the lobbying for the preservation of the past drew on an understanding that the incipient nation state had itself a past to preserve and that it was somehow significant. But at different times in the long history of the English Reformation, both the old (Gothic) and the new (Classical) might be seized on by different interest groups to support different ideas of how that past was shaped.

It has often been argued that for the Protestant group of the mid-16th century, the men in power at the court of Edward VI led by the Protector, the Duke of Somerset, a form of Classicism which sought to draw on inspiration directly from Italy was their way of marking a clarity of purpose that echoed their political and religious radicalism. Mid-century writers who supported Protestant reform looked to the Classical world for templates of good governance before the Popish despotism held sway over the Christian world.[21] It has equally been recently argued very forcefully that some generations later, in the political divisions that led to Civil War, the affirmed choice of Gothic, initially in texts but later manifest in a series of remarkable buildings at Oxford, was a way of stressing a radical challenge to royal power (which in its courtly manifestation had shown a Classical face to the world in its building patronage) by associating Gothic with long-held parliamentary privilege and freedoms.[22] Both these phenomena, mid-16th-century Classicism and 17th-century Gothic, can be argued therefore as very deliberate stylistic revivals, where references to a set of stylistic criteria different from the prevailing fashions of building of their time were important.

In the intervening period between the mid-16th century and the early 17th, Elizabethan building can be said to exhibit a more complex and negotiative role with respect to the past. Much of this appears to be directed towards underlining the impression that in a century of religious and political upheaval, some aspects of the building fabric of the country remained intact. Notwithstanding the few examples of new churches built in the Classical style, it seems that the consolidation of churches in the later 16th century took an extraordinarily conservative line, rebuilding towers where necessary (though recent historians have disputed hotly the reasons for this) and not showing signs of the very deliberate reinvention of medieval style favoured a few decades later.[23] Concerning secular architecture, however, much has been written on the refurbishment of castles and the construction of a handful of new, small versions of castles as the pleasure domes of a handful of early-17th-century patrons.[24] Although many of the medieval royal castles have been shown to be redundant at this period, it is interesting that amongst many of the old Tudor nobility (including some new families, such as the Howard dukes of Norfolk, who had assumed an old title of nobility the century before), great castles were maintained and renewed in the course of the 16th century.[25] Much evidence of this work has subsequently disappeared: that of the Fitzalans, earls of Arundel, at Arundel in Sussex, the Manners, lords Ros, at Belvoir in Leicestershire, the Percies, earls of Northumberland, at Alnwick in Northumberland – all major building works that were removed in the course of 19th-century refashioning. Yet there remain, along the ruinous curtain walls of the medieval castle, the Tudor chimneystacks from the modernisation by the dukes of Norfolk of the castle at Framlingham in Suffolk and the spectacular remains of the work of the third and fourth earls of Worcester at Raglan in Wales. The fact that all these peers also built newer houses on other parts of their estates and indeed in London, testifies to the fact that it was important to retain the castle's state, for the accommodation of the noble household in its entirety. The talismanic quality of the castle, no longer pretending to real defence but promoting the shadow of that earlier power for the sake of status, remained significant.[26]

And yet, as Girouard noted, one of the most striking things about the Elizabethan period is the frequent respect paid in great buildings to the recent past, to the power and achievements of Elizabeth's grandfather and father, Henry VII and Henry VIII.[27] Commentators such as William Harrison referred to Henry VIII as a great builder of royal palaces and coastal defences, emphasising a permanent legacy which thus offset any anxiety about the accompanying destruction of the patrimony following the Reformation of the 1530s.

Girouard noted the similarity of aspect between the early Tudor palace of Richmond and the west front of Burghley House, the last part of that great house completed for William Cecil in the 1580s and arguably the most conservative of its building campaigns.

We can put a gloss on Girouard's point here to suggest that his illustration of Richmond, the 17th-century view by Hollar, may itself be something of a reinvention, a heightening of the quality of 'Tudor' in its aspect as perceived by later eyes, which only underlines the point that the very act of looking at and recording buildings will reinforce preconceived notions of their historic significance and even exaggerate their chief stylistic qualities. In considerations of the Elizabethan cult of the past, it has been recognised that castles played a key role and that they held their greatest symbolic value when serving as stages for the enactment of loyalty in entertaining the Queen herself. Much has been made of the castle of Kenilworth, added to by Robert Dudley, Earl of Leicester, both between and especially immediately before the visits of Elizabeth there and the entertainments that took place on the ground between its medieval keep, new ranges of lodgings and new gatehouse, making new uses of the medieval layout.[28] Perhaps more revealing, however, shifting the venue to a great house and with reference to a more recent time, is the use of Cowdray, in West Sussex, for the visit of the Queen in 1591. The Catholic Anthony Browne, Viscount Montague, anxious to underline his loyalty to Queen and country, devised an entertainment to emphasise those qualities of rural continuity and connections with the English past that he, as owner, treasured and of which he, as loyal subject, saw her as embodying. The setting, of course, was a house no more than half a century old, built during the reign of Elizabeth's father, with an approach across water, a turreted gatehouse, and a varied skyline of building ranges. It must have struck just the right note of conservative building style alongside the traditional values expressed in the entertainment, of underlining the knowledge that all present would have shared, that it was Elizabeth's father who first raised the Browne family to the highest social level. 'Elizabethan

The Historiography of 'Elizabethan Gothic'

Gothic' can be said here to encompass a recent past whose buildings are already conjoined to the country's medieval building stock.[29]

    An early-20th-century image strikes the right note with which to conclude. One of the most striking wall paintings in St Stephen's Hall at the Palace of Westminster is the bright, fresco-coloured 1925-7 painting by Alfred Kingsley Lawrence of Queen Elizabeth commissioning Raleigh to sail for America in 1584, an image known to many through its wide illustration in a certain generation of history books and its influence on early cinematic representations of Elizabeth's life. In the top right-hand corner, two buildings evoke the period, but these are not 'modern' buildings, examples of the new, glittering multi-windowed houses of the Elizabethan age, but a semblance of the outer entry to Base Court at Hampton Court Palace (its gatehouse in its later, truncated

Cowdray House, Sussex, west front, gutted by fire in 1793 (*Country Life Picture Library*).

Opposite top: Burghley House, Northamptonshire, west front (*Country Life Picture Library*).

Opposite below: Richmond Palace, Surrey by Wenceslaus Hollar (*Ashmolean Museum*).

Alfred Kingsley Lawrence, Queen Elizabeth commissioning Raleigh to sail for America (*Palace of Westminster, London*).

version) and a high, windowless, evocative castle (not even Windsor, where Elizabeth carried out some of her few extensive royal domestic building works). Here the artist recognised that among the most familiar buildings to the Elizabethan court were those of both a distant and a recent past, and all treated with much veneration.

Notes

1 Andrea Fredericksen, 'Parliament's Genius Loci: The Politics of Place after the 1834 Fire', in *The Houses of Parliament: History, Art, Architecture*, with an introduction by Christine Riding and Jacqueline Riding (London, 2000), pp. 99-111.

2 Mark Girouard, 'Elizabethan Architecture and the Gothic Tradition', *Architectural History*, 6 (1963), pp. 23-38.

3 The most useful discussions of the historiography of Gothic and Gothic Revival are E. S. de Beer, 'Gothic: Origin and Diffusion of the Term; the Idea of Style in Architecture', *Journal of the Warburg and Courtauld Institutes*, 11 (1948), pp. 143-62; Peter Frankl, *The Gothic. Literary Sources and Interpretations through Eight Centuries* (Princeton, 1960); Stuart Piggott, *Ruins in a Landscape. Essays in Antiquarianism* (Edinburgh, 1976); Thomas Cocke, 'The Wheel of Fortune: the Appreciation of Gothic since the Middle Ages', in *The Age of Chivalry. Art in Plantagenet England 1200-1400*, edited by

Jonathan Alexander and Paul Binski (London, 1987), pp. 183-91; Chris Brooks, *The Gothic Revival* (London, 1999).

4 Eric Mercer's comments on panelling of this period in *English Art 1553-1625* (Oxford, 1962), pp. 104-8, remain illuminating and influential.

5 The Haynes Grange Room was last explored in a substantial way by Mark Girouard, 'The Haynes Grange Room', in *Town and Country* (New Haven and London, 1992), pp. 173-86. As part of the reinstallation of part of the room in the British Galleries at the Victoria and Albert Museum in 2001, new investigations were carried out on the room's history and structure. The dating of the ornament print which is the source for the fireplace as 1585 is thanks to Peter Führing (personal communication with Michael Snodin, Victoria and Albert Museum).

6 Brooks, op. cit. [note 3].

7 C. J. Richardson, *Observations on the Architecture of England during the Reigns of Queen Elizabeth and King James I* (London, 1837), p. 8.

8 J. B. Waring, 'Elizabethan Ornament' in Owen Jones, *The Grammar of Ornament* (London, 1856), p. 133.

9 Nikolaus Pevsner and Alexandra Wedgwood, *The Buildings of England: Warwickshire* (Harmondsworth, 1966), p. 227. A 1558 date for the completion of the house (rather than the beginning of the building campaign, as Pevsner suggest) is taken from *Charlecote Park* (National Trust guidebook, London, 1996), accepting more recent views that the house was begun when Thomas Lucy inherited in 1551. Heraldic glass was installed in 1558.

10 Mercer, op. cit. [note 4]; John Summerson, *Architecture in Britain 1530-1830* (Harmondsworth, 1953 and subsequent editions); Girouard, op. cit. [note 2] and the same author's *Robert Smythson and the Elizabethan Country House* (New Haven and London, 1983).

11 Deborah Howard, 'The Protestant Renaissance', *Architectural Heritage: the Journal of the Architectural Heritage Society of Scotland*, 9 (1998), pp. 1-15.

12 Timothy Mowl, *Elizabethan and Jacobean Style* (London, 1993).

13 Giorgio Vasari, *Lives of the Artists*, translated by George Bull (Harmondsworth, 1965), p. 386.

14 Stephen Orgel and Roy Strong, *Inigo Jones: the Theatre of the Stuart Court* (Los Angeles, 1973), volume 1, p. 160.

15 M. F. S. Hervey, *The Life, Correspondence and Collections of Thomas Howard, Earl of Arundel* (Cambridge, 1921), p. 451.

16 John Evelyn, 'Account of Architects and Architecture', appendix to his translation of *Parallèle de l'architecture antique et de la*

moderne by Roland de Fréart (London, 1707).

17 *The Diary of John Evelyn*, edited by E. S. de Beer, (Oxford, 1959), pp. 353, 543.

18 Sebastiano Serlio, *The Five Books of Architecture*, reprint of the 1611 edition of Robert Peake (New York, 1982), second book, third chapter, folio 25.

19 For the incidence of Serlio and other foreign treatises in English libraries, see Lucy Gent, *Picture and Poetry, 1560-1620* (Leamington Spa, 1981). On the history of editions of Serlio in England, see Eileen Harris, assisted by Nicholas Savage, *British Architectural Books and Writers 1556-1785* (Cambridge, 1990), pp. 414-17.

20 *Architecture de Philibert de l'Orme ...,* edited by Pierre Mardaga from the 1648 Rouen edition (Brussels, 1981), IV, chapt. X.

21 Maurice Howard, 'Self-fashioning and the Classical Moment in mid-16th century English Architecture', in *Renaissance Bodies*, edited by Lucy Gent and Nigel Llewellyn (London, 1990), pp. 198-217.

22 Brooks, op. cit. [note 3].

23 On the dispute about the rebuilding of church towers, see A. Woodger, 'Post-Reformation Mixed Gothic in Huntingdonshire Church Towers and its Campanological Associations', *Archaeological Journal*, 141 (1984), pp. 269-308; G. W. Bernard, 'The Dating of Church Towers: Huntingdonshire Re-examined', *Archaeological Journal*, 149 (1992), pp. 344-50.

24 Principally, Lulworth, Ruppera and Bolsover; see Girouard (1983), op. cit. [note 10] chapter 6.

25 On the decline of royal castles, see Howard Colvin, 'Castles and Government in Tudor England', *English Historical Review*, 83 (1969), pp. 125-39; *History of the King's Works*, volume 4 (London, 1982).

26 A recent thought-provoking reassessment of the castle in Tudor England is Matthew Johnson, 'Reconstructing Castles and Refashioning Identities in Renaissance England', in *The Familiar Past? Archaeologies of Later Historical Britain*, edited by Sarah Tarlow and Susie West (London and New York, 1999), pp. 69-86.

27 Girouard, op. cit. [note 2].

28 Roy Strong, *The Cult of Elizabeth* (London, 1977); Jean Wilson, *Entertainments for Elizabeth I* (Totowa, N.J., 1980).

29 Charles Curtis Bright, 'Caressing the Great: Viscount Montague's Entertainment of Elizabeth at Cowdray, 1591', *Sussex Archaeological Collections*, 127 (1989), pp. 147-66.

3

'The Wrong Things at the Wrong Time'
17th–Century Gothic churches

'The Wrong Things at the Wrong Time' 17th-Century Gothic churches

'The Wrong Things at the Wrong Time'
17th-Century Gothic churches

Timothy Mowl

MANY NOSTALGIC tears have been shed over an inscription set above the door of the Leicestershire church of Holy Trinity, Staunton Harold, which was built in 1653 at the dead heart of the Commonwealth: 'When all things sacred were throughout ye nation Either demollisht or profaned Sir Robert Shirley Barronet Founded this Church whose singular praise it is to have done the best things in ye worst times And hoped them in the most callamitous. The Righteous shall be had in everlasting remembrance.'

When the head of the Church of England was a secret Roman Catholic who had, for political advantage, recently signed the Covenant as a Scottish Presbyterian, the temptation must have been strong to look backwards to the cosy village pieties which that reasonably convincing recreation of a Perpendicular Gothic church of perhaps 1450 represents. It should be remembered too that the inscription itself is not Commonwealth in date, but a post-Restoration declaration of militant and self-satisfied Cavalier conservatism. The medieval illusion of the structure is not perfect. Sir Robert's church is high, wide and handsome, but too short in the nave for the bold profile of its tower. A real Gothic church would not have encased its octagonal columns in geometric wooden panelling almost up to the level of the capitals, and the roof of the nave betrays that almost Muslim horror which 17th-century Protestants tended to feel for any representation of the human form divine. Where a 15th-century builder would have supported roof beams with ranks of carved wooden angels, Sir Robert's architect raised a flat ceiling and called in journeymen painters, Samuell and Zachary Kyrk, to daub an abstract composition of cloudy forms where the mere Hebrew name of God is about to create order from primeval chaos.[1]

Opposite:
South elevation, St Mary, Warwick 1695 (*Author*).

With these reservations, the gesture of Staunton Harold church is both moving and blindly reactionary. Shirley would pay for his loyalty to a threatened faith by imprisonment in the Tower, where he died in 1656, before the chancel of his Holy Trinity had been completed. A few Classical details, demi-columns and drapes, would creep into post-Restoration (1662-5) work on the porch; but in 1653 there had only been one way for a beleaguered Anglican squire to look for architectural guidance, and that was backwards. He did not turn to Calvinist or Lutheran models, such as there were, nor to the attractive prototypes of Italian and French Catholicism, but to an insular stylistic tradition and the comfort of familiar ecclesiastical forms. By choosing Richard Shepherd (died 1673) from a family of master masons from near Repton, Derbyshire, as his architect, Sir Robert ensured a deadening stylistic conservatism.

Unfortunately it was not just during the grim 1650s, but for the best part of the entire, dogma-obsessed 17th century, that the Church of England remained so paranoid about the Baroque associations of continental Catholicism, so unsure of its own identity and of any positive architectural way forward, that it lapsed into the dreariest kind of stylistic conservatism.

Twenty-five years earlier, another inscription had been carved over another church door, this time a cathedral door, a brand new Anglican cathedral of the 17th century; and it ran: 'If stones could speak then London's prayse should sound/Who built this church and cittie from the grounde'. But the reach of Anglican architectural ambitions in 1628, when William Parrott designed and built Londonderry's new cathedral of St Columb with £4,000 from the London Irish Society, extended only to an interior of six bays of octagonal piers, its chancel undemarcated, and the whole simple rectangle lit by cusped lancets under segmental hood moulds.[2] Parrott's original cathedral only went as far as the projecting turrets at the end of the aisles of the present structure. While on the continent, Classical Mannerism was surging into the theatrical concaves and convexes of Carlo Maderna and Pietro da Cortona's Baroque, Anglicans were raising as a cathedral a building so limited that an English village of the

'The Wrong Things at the Wrong Time' 17th-Century Gothic churches

St Columb
Cathedral,
Londonderry 1628
(*Author*).

15th century would not have found it remarkable or praise-
worthy.

Back in 1948, Sir Howard Colvin wrote a fascinating
detective essay to examine the puzzling interface of Gothic
Survival and Gothic Revival.[3] Colvin was considering their
dated work to see whether country masons, such as the
Woodwards in the Cotswolds, essentially provincial figures,
actually spanned in their lifetimes the gap between Gothic as
a living tradition of architectural design and Gothic with a
'k', the sophisticated new style of eclectic revival pioneered
by such 18th-century designers as Hawksmoor, Kent,
Langley and Miller. The evidence was not conclusive and,
rather than returning to yet another consideration of the
links between 17th- and 18th-century Gothic, this study will
examine the complex varieties of 17th-century Gothic itself
in the perspective of the preceding three centuries. This,
looking backward, is unavoidable, as 17th-century Gothic
was for the most part a debased Perpendicular Gothic, and
the Perpendicular style itself appears to have had its blighted
origins in the Black Death, raging in the late 1340s. That
plague wiped out so many skilled craftsmen that an inferior
'do-it-by-numbers' Gothic had to take over from the glorious inventions and curvilinearity of Decorated Gothic,
almost before the Decorated style had really gained momen-
tum.[4]

It was Nikolaus Pevsner, a cool-hearted German

outsider, who had the detachment to point out what loyal, over-reverent English writers on medieval architecture had never dared to articulate: that Perpendicular Gothic tended to a mechanical repetition of often unattractive motifs.[5] It relied on trefoil- and quatrefoil-headed window lights with the same trefoil-headed panelling netted across its church walls and towers, while unaspiring four-centred arches were ranged boringly in many hundred clerestories of Cotswold and East Anglian 'wool' churches. Even King's College Chapel, Cambridge, repeated the same unit of construction over and over again without variation or cross vistas, its side chapels needlessly excluded from the central space, so that the impact, while admittedly sublime, is as unsubtle as that of Tate Modern and would be almost as chilling were it not for the glass, which had to be Flemish, as native English glaziers were, by the time Henry VIII came to the throne, producing washed-out designs with too much clear glass for any dramatic interior lighting.

Perpendicular Gothic was trapped in ugly right angles of tracery, its mouldings are usually coarse, the capitals of its columns are conventionally stylized and stone carving of any vitality or inspiration is a rarity. To compound the stylistic staleness, while Early English and Decorated each lasted barely a century, Perpendicular had already laboured on for two centuries by the time Henry dissolved the monasteries. Yet, because the king and his children separated English culture from that of the continent at precisely the point when the Italian Renaissance should have been getting through to an insular culture, England had to make do with Perpendicular, increasingly watered down and uninspired, for another century and a half. If the Great Fire of London had not intervened to give Christopher Wren his big opportunity it might have stumbled on even longer.

It is manifestly not the purpose of this chapter to overload English 17th-century Gothic churches with praise; but they are a significant phenomenon which cannot be ignored. There are many more of them than is usually supposed (six or seven in most counties except Norfolk, together with one Irish cathedral and half of Bath Abbey), so their existence does usefully underline that tragic irresolution in English architectural development which the 17th century represents. In the short space of 75 years the country had experimented with Smythson's revived Gothic, Jacobean fantasy houses, Inigo Jones's Palladianism, Artisan Mannerism, Puritan Minimalism and bland Charles II Dutch Classicism, yet through all those changes church builders had laboured on in a tired and unenterprising survival Gothic. That was the stylistic price paid for becoming an isolated Protestant island.

If direction in church building was to be looked for, as the nation tried to make up its mind on matters of church ritual, then the places where a lead might have been expected were first London and then Oxford and Cambridge. It was the principal function of the two universities at the time to educate new men to staff the 9,000 clergy servicing England's 9,244 parishes, and to counter the roughly 500-strong force of Catholic priests, some of them Jesuits, working, not always as furtively as popular opinion now assumes, for the reconversion of England. [6]

There are no reliable figures for the Recusant population of 17th-century England. The English were never converted emotionally into the doctrines and the rituals of the Church of England. Indeed the Elizabethan State regarded itself as being in the business of enforcing religious conformity to its bureaucratic structures, not as being responsible for converting the English to a new faith. There was no consensus in either Church or State as to what any new faith might be. Religious flux was the very spirit and expectation of the times.[7] Political pressures, the selfish interest of the new aristocracy and a system of Elizabethan fines created a captive congregation. 'Church Papists', as superficial conformists were called, could still have been in a majority as late as 1610. Dramatic accounts of priest's holes and details of the torture and execution of a few over-bold Jesuit martyrs, tend to exaggerate the intolerance of the period. Even after the Gunpowder Plot of 1605 most Catholics in this country continued to enjoy a relative calm of toleration. The King's wife, Anne of Denmark, was a closet Catholic, James's own mother had been a Catholic martyr and the family of the King's favourite, the Duke of Buckingham, virtually all converted to Catholicism.[8] It was the Popish Plot of 1683 that really stirred up anti-Papalism in the national psyche, and even then a register of Catholic gentry in Herefordshire drawn up in the mid–18th century reveals that half the county's upper class was still Recusant.[9]

That figure of 9,000 Church of England clergy is the key. Who trained them and who supervised their practice? More relevantly, who appointed them to their comfortable posts? The answer to the last question has to be the local landowner, and all accounts agree that the gentry, being able to pay church fines, were more Catholic than their peasantry; and gentry wives even more than gentry husbands, as the men tended to conform in order to qualify for the position and influence of a local magistrate.[10] So how many of the 9,000 ministers who served them in their churches were facing both ways religiously, delivering Prayer Book services on Sundays, but conducting, or turning a blind eye to, the Catholic Mass in side chapels? Protestant bishops competed to offer benefices to any Catholic priest willing to make a token conversion to the Church of England, while some priests converted because of their dislike of the Jesuits working in their midst. Archbishop Abbot put a renegade Catholic priest, John Copley, into the vicarage of Bethersden and then into the richer rectory of Pluckley, both in Kent. Archbishop Whitgift gave livings to four other renegades. Two priests, Ralph Ithell and Robert Fisher, converted because of their dislike of Jesuit faction.[11] The interesting question is which services are these priests most likely to have conducted – the Mass or Holy Communion? Depending upon the religious bias of their new patrons, they may have conducted both.

A significant number of family chapels were added to churches at this period, usually sited at right angles to the nave so that they were out of sight of the congregation, and most of them with private entrances at the side aisle. The squire of a parish would normally expect to make a state entrance among his tenants by the main door. Did those private doors give access for the continuation, among family tombs, of prayers for the dead or stealthy masses celebrated by facing-both-ways vicars eager to oblige their patrons? At St Leonard, Beoley in Worcestershire the Catholic squire,

Side chapel,
St Leonard, Beoley,
Worcestershire
c. 1602 (*Author*).

Ralph Sheldon, built a sturdy side chapel of about 1602 which still has the stone altar at which he offered prayers for his ancestors.[12] For the style of the chapel he appears to have deliberately revived the forms of Perpendicular Gothic, merely rounding the point of its east window, perhaps in a vague gesture to Renaissance forms on the continent .What was the real function of the Berkeley Chapel of 1614, built next to the sanctuary at All Saints, Spetchley, again in Worcestershire, a notably Recusant county?[13] At their enforced Prayer Book services Sir Richard Shireburn blocked his ears with wool, Sir Nicholas Gerard loudly recited Latin psalms and Sir Thomas Cornwallis contemptuously read a Lady Psalter.[14] If they had been tucked away out of sight in a new side chapel all these embarrassments could have been avoided. A 17th-century side chapel should be seen as at least a possible indication of Recusancy.[15]

Until the Great Fire of 1666, London gave an uncertain lead. Lincoln's Inn's new chapel went up in 1619-23. Inigo Jones had been consulted, but what the lawyers built was Gothic Perpendicular with just the Tuscan columns as a Classical gesture in its open undercroft. Then came St Katherine Cree of 1628-31. John Newman has suggested a link here with St Mary, Goudhurst in Kent, where the mason Edward Kinsman was active on the tower between 1638 and 1640.[16]

Holy Trinity, Leweston, Dorset, 1616 (*Author*).

But a group of Dorset churches all featured, often insistently, the three-light window which seems to have been late Gothic's response to Classicism's three-part Venetian or Serlian motif before it appeared in churches of the capital. A number of local gentry living around Sherborne - Sir Thomas Freke, Sir Robert Napier and Sir John Fitzjames - seem to have skimmed the pages of Serlio and approved this very conservative Gothic response to it. Sir Robert Napier's family chapel attached to St Andrew, Minterne Magna was built in 1610, long before Katherine Cree, but the jewel of this Dorset cluster is Fitzjames's Holy Trinity, Leweston, which, although a parish church, stands like a private chapel in the shadow of the hall, far from the village. All its windows are of the three-light type, except the east window. Its proportions are entirely un-medieval, boxy and experimental, like the tower of St Hippolyte, Ryme Intrinseca in the adjacent parish, which also has three-light windows in the body of the church. This quality of boxy compression is best expressed in the last of this group, St Lawrence, Folke of 1628, where a Classical fixation with symmetry lies behind the Gothic whole. These three-light windows were, in fact,

common enough in the period, a sign of domestic and ecclesiastical forms merging. Katherine Cree was not the only London church featuring them. The lost church of St Gregory, next to Old St Paul's, had the same three-light windows, and Katherine Cree itself was to be the model for a church at Berwick upon Tweed which the Mercers' Company of London paid to have built as a Puritan tabernacle between 1649 and 1657.[17]

St Lawrence, Folke, Dorset 1628 (*Author*).

Although Katherine Cree adopted the Dorset three-light windows for its side elevations in that compromise style, its vault imitates Gothic forms with non-structural plaster ribs and for its east window the great Gothic rose within a rectangle of the retrochoir of Old St Paul's was copied. Yet its interior arcades have accurate Corinthian capitals and correctly coffered Classical soffits, making it an uneasy, schizoid building.

London would have to wait 60 years before an architect, Christopher Wren – or possibly the mason-surveyor John Oliver – was sufficiently sure of his Classical vocabulary to abandon it almost completely and indulge himself with the design of St Mary Aldermary, in uninhibited

Screen, Bishop
Auckland Chapel,
County Durham
1664 (*Author*).

Gothic pastiche, where fan-vaulting works around saucer domes above arcades of elegant, slimline Perpendicular arches.[18] This deliciously frivolous confection was prophetic. English patrons and designers of the next century were to prefer a native filigree Gothic with a 'k' to the contemporary French rococo.

Cambridge has only one 17th-century Gothic chapel, that at Peterhouse of 1632, but indirectly it may have given John Cosin the taste for that stylistically free-for all Jacobean-Gothic which was to make his reign as Bishop of Durham so productive, though more in the way of woodwork than of stonework.

In answer to the vexed question – 'Is Cosin's work in Durham Gothic Survival or Gothic Revival?' – one point can be made. Cosin's canopied choir and screen at Brancepeth, put up when he was rector there after 1626 and before the Civil War, were far more committedly Gothic than the screen which he raised after the Civil War in the chapel of Bishop Auckland Castle, where Renaissance motifs are decidedly prevalent. The logic of that shift is that his work was Gothic Survival, not Revival; he was, later in his career, heading away from Gothic rather than deeper into it.

Brancepeth was tragically gutted in 1999, but the furnishings, screen, choir stalls and panelling of the sanctuary at St Edmund, Sedgefield were designed closely on the Brancepeth model after 1667 by Cosin's son-in-law, the

rector Dennis Granville. In contrast, on the far more exuberant screen at Bishop Auckland, Cosin's own private chapel, it requires an effort to pick out the Gothic detail from the Carolean Renaissance work. In Durham Cathedral itself, the survival-revival question gets no clear answer. The Cosin canopies in the choir are convincing Perpendicular Gothic in profile, though rather coarsely detailed, while the great font cover supports its towering Gothic canopy on openly Renaissance columns.[19]

Lincoln College chapel, Oxford, 1629-31 (*Author*).

There was far more Gothic building in the colleges of Oxford than those of Cambridge and it was there that something close to a fourth style of Gothic - slick, sinuous and consciously deviant - very nearly emerged as a national church style. Its tracery inclined to the mandorla oval, vertically or horizontally sited. A chronological list of such instances will reveal a certain drive to escape from the Perpendicular to an uncusped pattern-making, apparently inspired by Jacobean strapwork. Wadham, of 1610-13, first set the pattern. There the Arnold brothers, William and Edward, brought out from Somerset as master masons, designed with an obsessive symmetry, even to the point of providing one false door on the right of the central main entrance. Their

The vault of
Brasenose College
chapel, Oxford,
1659-66 (*Author*).

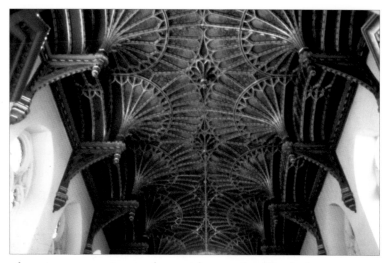

elevations contrive to be neither truly Classical nor accurately Gothic, but they made a token gesture to Classicism – that of a precocious schoolboy rather than an architect – with a tower of the orders. In the same year, 1610, an even bigger tower was going up across the road at the Schools, again an otherwise symmetrical Gothic building. Oriel (1620-42) came next: Wadham repeated but with a skyline of shaped gables. Then there was Lincoln chapel of 1629-31. Brasenose (1659-66) was an ambitious attempt to fuse Gothic and Baroque, but blighted, as a copyable influence, by its Commonwealth dating and its amateurish setting of the two styles side-by-side with broken pediments over Gothic points, rather than fusing them together in basic Baroque rhythms.[20] John Jackson, its architect, enjoyed Gothic detail too much, as his wood and plaster vault reveals, to subsume its fans within the rectangles of a conventional Classical ceiling. Lastly, University College chapel of 1666 has more mandorla tracery.

The odd one out in the sequence is Lincoln chapel, a completely authentic Perpendicular design of 1629, where the illusion of the 15th century is only spoilt by the superb, 17th-century Van Linge glass, and of course the woodwork, wood carvers of this period usually being a century ahead of stone carvers in their designs. Lincoln chapel was paid for by Archbishop Laud's great rival, Bishop Williams of Lincoln, later Archbishop of York. Williams epitomises the conflicts of Charles I's reign. Open minded and forward thinking in science, he was a friend of Samuel Hartlib (lending him an episcopal palace in which to teach the new agricultural theory of crop rotation with new improved fodder like sainfoin) and brought Comenius over from Bohemia for a year to proselytize for Pansophism, yet his churchmanship was right-wing.[21] When he was Dean of Westminster a French abbot had congratulated him on ritual so splendid that it equalled that of Rome.[22] Williams's English contemporaries were nervously aware of these Romish tendencies. Garrard wrote that Lincoln chapel's 'communion table, pulpit and an excellent fair screen, all of cedar ... gives such an odiferous smell that holy water in the Romish churches doth not exceed it, let them use what they can to perfume it'.[23] Williams's deployment of a pure Perpendicular style at Lincoln College should be seen as a sophisticated statement of High Anglican politics.

Mention of the glass in the chapel of Lincoln College is a reminder of the sad decline of Gothic stained glass in England during this period and of the need to import the Dutch Van Linges to glaze 17th-century Oxford. There is a telling demonstration of that decline in the glass supplied to the churches of two neighbouring parishes in Herefordshire during the 17th century. The glass in the east window of St Tysilio, Sellack, was put together for Richard Scudamore from partly contemporary, partly 15th- and 16th-century pieces in 1630.[24] That was just before Louis XIII invaded Lorraine and destroyed the last coloured or pot-glass manufacturies. The Sellack window is a highly acceptable pastiche of the best medieval, glass with good colours and clear images. Christ crucified (with blood-red pot glass) at the top is authentic 17th-century work. The canopies are a

East window, St Tysilio, Sellack, Herefordshire, 1630 (*Author*).

East window,
St Mary, Foy,
Herefordshire,
1673 (*Author*).

fair, if geometric, attempt at Gothic authenticity. In the Nativity scene, Mary, Joseph and the Three Kings are shown with the ox and the ass; St Catherine is on their right.

John Abrahall of Foy, in the next parish, admired the Scudamore gift so much that he left property in his will of 1640 to have made 'a fayer windowe contayning three lights and there place the same after the same manner as such a windowe is placed in the church of Sellack'.[25] But in 1673, while the Foy mason could make a good copy of the Sellack mason's Decorated-style tracery, the local glazier, lacking the pot-glass of Lorraine, could achieve only a poor ghost of the glass at Sellack. His colours have grown thin, the drawing is uncertain, the leading sometimes crude; only the ox and the ass still come out clearly. What had happened is that the art of English stained glass had been sidelined by the new painted glass from the Low Countries with its richer, deeper colours and alien drawing style.

In this depressing decline of crafts it is satisfying, just occasionally, to come across an ecclesiastical equivalent of Robert Smythson's great revival of Perpendicular Gothic forms in such houses as Hardwick Hall and Wootton Lodge. That the Renaissance and the Gothic could also profitably co-exist within churches is demonstrated in two neighbouring Somerset parishes: Axbridge at the foot of the Mendips, and East Brent out in the Somerset levels. In both churches the roofs are triumphs of this 17th-century compromise style.

St John Baptist, Axbridge came first. In 1636 the substantial cruciform town church was roofed, originally without interruption from east to west end, with an astonishing

Detail of ceiling,
St John Baptist,
Axbridge,
Somerset, 1636
(*Author*).

nostalgia for the medieval, all the thin-ribbed Jacobean ribs of the patterning being cusped in a deliberate Gothic gesture. The 'local' man who was paid £10. 5s. 0d. for his work was almost certainly the same plasterer who roofed the stairs at Barrow Gurney Court, a few miles to the north, with the same cusping.[26] The churchwardens of St Mary, East Brent, William Morrish and Nicolas Isgar, had just, in 1635, added a west gallery to their church and were clearly so impressed by the spatial unity which Axbridge had gained by replacing wooden beams with unifying plaster that they employed the same team to roof their own rather less regular space.

These two plaster roofs seem isolated now, but this may be because they were the kind of church feature that the Victorians inclined to replace with something darker and more authentically medieval. Both churches are in the diocese of Bath and Wells, and Bath Abbey, referred to earlier, had, until Scott replaced it with stone fan vaulting in 1864, a huge plaster vault of about 1614 raised by Bishop Montague. A section of it still survives in the clergy vestry and that could well have been the inspiration for Axbridge. Of equal interest are the large aisle windows of this overlit, lantern-like church, some of which have preserved their original tracery – plain, uncusped nets – in sharp contrast to the standard cusped Perpendicular tracery which Scott inserted in the other openings. The Abbey has a complex building history dating back to 1499 and the fan vaulting of its south transept

West window,
Low Ham, Somerset
(*Author*).

is a piece of major Gothic engineering of the reign of James I, so it is unlikely that these severe net traceries date back to Henry VII's reign. An early-17th-century date is more probable. That plasterers should add cusping at Axbridge while masons were abandoning cusping at Bath Abbey is a perversity of stylistic direction, but typical of the decadent and uncertain stylistic course of 17th-century Gothic design.

A mason or architect's personal signature in a church is most clearly written on its window tracery. Oxford has its strapwork mandorlas and there seems to have been another individual hand designing in the West Country just before the outbreak of the Civil War, first at Low Ham and then in Plymouth. But then, rather improbably, the same architect, who could perhaps be called the 'Master of the Radiant Star Tracery', appears to have come out of retirement after the Civil War to redesign the great west window of Lichfield Cathedral, which had been half-ruined in the Civil War sieges of 1643 and 1646.

Low Ham is a lost church that has become quite famous for its dramatic obscurity. It stands isolated in the middle of a field next to an untidy farmyard, with only a few ridges up the hillside above it to indicate where its parent manor house once stood. There was a medieval church on the site before Sir Edward Hext, who died in 1623, is supposed to have begun the present building. Another possibility is that it was rebuilt, as a faithful duty, by his wife, who died in 1633. Husband and wife lie side by side in the north aisle. The proportions of the church, like those of the later Staunton Harold, are subtly wrong. It is a little too short for its height as if someone had been trying to include all the usual medieval village church features before the money ran out. There is for instance a priest's door which can never have

Above: Charles Church, Plymouth 1641-3 (*Author*).

led anywhere, but the builder knew that a priest was supposed to need his own entrance so he included one. The tracery of several windows features radiant star bursts, a distinctive and satisfying motif.

To complicate Low Ham's complexity there was, according to the county's historian John Collinson, a second building phase after the Civil War in 1668.[27] So was the admonitory text (Proverbs, Chapter 24, verse 21) on the quite elaborate rood screen a prophecy or an afterthought: 'My sonne fear God and the King and meddle not with them that are given to change'? I believe the cherubs of its carving are of Charles I's period, not Charles II's, and the rood screen is entirely 17th century. Carpenters of the 15th century are unlikely to have made such a botched job of the perforations.

After Low Ham came the Charles Church, Plymouth, which, though now a blitzed and gutted ruin in the middle of a busy roundabout, must still be ranked as the second most ambitious Gothic church of the entire 17th century. The radiant star tracery features boldly in all three windows at its east end and in two at its west. The body of the church is dated 1643 but services were being held as early as 1641, so it is Caroline in dating, not Commonwealth.[28] Whoever designed the body of the church meant it to suggest a complex medieval building history. The nave arcades copy those of Plymouth's parish church and while the larger windows are in this radiant star-burst version of Decorated Gothic tracery, the aisle windows and the porch are accurately Perpendicular Gothic in their detail. There is no other church of the period remotely similar in its scale or its authentic medieval profile. The king may have taken a personal interest because of the dedication, but which architect in court circles would have been capable of such an elaborate, almost scholarly, deception in the Gothic?

King Charles I is not usually credited with a keen sense of humour, but it seems possible that Plymouth's Charles Church was a gesture and even a royal joke at the Puritans' expense. The town's ardently Puritan, Parliamentary citizens had been agitating for a second church and parish for years. Then when Charles consented to their appeals he stipulated that, as a token of loyalty, it should be dedicated to him, a premature saint. He may also have required an elaborately traditional design, High Church and focused on an east-end altar, which would not have been to the taste of a Puritan congregation. Plymouth did, however, have the last laugh when Charles became a real martyr if not an actual saint, while the congregation built a huge pulpit in the middle of the church with galleries all round it as in a nonconformist chapel. Exactly the same thing was happening to Holy Trinity, Berwick upon Tweed at just the same time.

The last grand appearance of the radiant star tracery was in the west window of Lichfield Cathedral, built during its major restoration, post-1664, but if there is a link between this tracery and that of Low Ham (c. 1620s) and Plymouth (1640), it has yet to be demonstrated.[29] The other tracery connection, that of the mandorlas, could be more easily explained by an Oxford connection through individual vicars.

A survey of some random examples of 17th-century church restorations reveals much of individual interest, but few signs of any emerging stylistic consistency. At St Leonard, Apethorpe, Northamptonshire, the Mildmay chapel of 1621 offers a dim Perpendicular Gothic container for staggering Baroque monuments that cry out for a Baroque chapel to set

them off. St Mary, Chiddingstone and St John Evangelist, Groombridge are both in Kent and both of exactly the same date – 1629 – but they still make no stylistic links with each other. St Mary, Leighton Bromswold's tower escaped the Gothic, but came nowhere near the Baroque. Its fenestration of 1634, attractively sleek, does hint at that fourth-period Gothic of the Oxford mandorlas. St Dionysius, Kelmarsh, Northamptonshire, of 1639 has an east window with a pure Oxford-style mandorla; while Holy Trinity, Rothwell's graceful infilling of spherical triangles, in windows inserted after a 17th-century demolition of side chapels, could be mistaken for Batty Langley designs of the 1740s. At St Saviour, Foremark, Derbyshire, Sir Francis Burdett's new church of 1662 has five lights under segmental hoodmoulds in a grudging imitation of Perpendicular Gothic. St Mary, Uffington, Berkshire has an unusual side chapel or tomb recess. John Deane is recorded as having built it for £25 in 1677, but without that information it could easily be taken for Arts and Crafts work of about 1905.[30] Its brazen geometry supports the claim that the equally geometric flint-work on the east end of Holy Trinity, Barsham, Suffolk, which is known to have been in place at the start of the 18th century, was work of 1633.[31]

St Mary, Newent in Gloucestershire, a monstrous, fascinating rebuild of 1675-9, is near the end of this Gothic line. The chancel and Lady chapel had survived the collapse of the nave and the vicar wanted a big, open preaching theatre with tiered seating facing a pulpit where a north aisle would normally have been sited. Two masons, Francis Jones of Hasfield and James Hill of Cheltenham, built and fenestrated the strange new arena.[32] A carpenter, Edward Taylor, who had worked with Wren on his flat roof for the Sheldonian in Oxford, devised another enormous flat roof to cover a completely uninterrupted area. Photographs quite fail to convey the scale of it all, but giant Ionic pilasters articulate the links with the surviving Gothic choir and side chapels and there has been a Puritan reduction of Gothic tracery to mere uncusped nets, not unlike those at Bath Abbey. Work was completed in 1679 and in that year the same masons, Francis Jones and James Hill, began creating at St Mary, Monnington-on-Wye, Herefordshire, the perfect Puritan village church. It has an interior of quiet charm with the same simplified tracery that they provided for Newent. Monnington, which can with an effort be described as Gothic, should be the end of the story, but 17th-century Gothic had one last unpredictable surprise in reserve.

With the exception of Wren's City churches and a few, rare, provincial churches, such as St Mary, Ingestre, Staffordshire of 1676 and St Mary Magdalene, Willen, Buckinghamshire of 1679–80, England had contrived to miss out on the dramatic control of space and the theatricality of the continental Baroque until, at the century's very last gasp, in 1694, a fire consumed the nave, tower and transepts of Warwick parish church, leaving the townspeople with the problem of how to rebuild while retaining the old, ugly chancel and the splendid Beauchamp Chapel to its south. Wren offered a design, but it was rejected and Sir William Wilson, a second-rate sculptor who had been knighted merely for the achievement of marrying a rich widow, was given the commission. He had little previous experience as an architect and none as a church builder. This shows in his tower, which jerks up to a height of 117 feet in a series of clumsily related stages. It nevertheless makes a superb street feature, acting as a giant *porte cochère*, striding out on arches over an intersection of roads while, from any distance, its sheer, gaunt height pulls the whole townscape together.

It is, however, the interior of the church which baffles and delights a visitor by its complete un-Englishness.[33] The entire luminous space of nave and barely differentiated transepts opens out as instant theatre. Nothing is familiar. It is a hall church. The massive columns have graceful acanthus capitals whose arches support without interval the broad plaster vault and Wilson's enormous windows flood the space with light. Two tiers of tracery, like those of Monnington hugely amplified, rise to giant vertical mandorlas. There is little then left to explore, unless the visitor dives down into the hidden Beauchamp Chapel or enters the uninviting dark tunnel of the chancel. In a sense, Gothic has been tamed to realise that Puritan preaching space towards which Newent had been striving, yet it has been achieved with all the numinous consequence of a small cathedral.

Wilson's success at St Mary's, Warwick is frustrating. It suggests what England could and should have been exploring right through that irresolute, wasted century. When considering the historic course of English ecclesiastical architecture it is a mistake to assume that all developments have always been for the best in a right little, tight little island. Until Wren and Hawksmoor began working in the fire-ravaged City of London parishes, church building in the 17th century has to be seen as long catalogue of undirected conservatism. When English architects and builders could and should have been exploring the spatial excitements of the Italian or German Baroque, they continued for 66 years in a clapped-out village Perpendicular Gothic which should have been abandoned in 1550 at the very latest.

The traumas suffered by the Church of England during the 17th century appear to have trapped its clergy in a nervous conservatism, which Wren's superb essay in French neo-Classsicism at St Paul's did curiously little to invigorate. Moreover, his, Nicholas Hawksmoor's and Thomas Archer's London churches were never widely imitated in provincial counties already over-stocked with survivals from medieval Catholic Christianity. It would be left to James Gibbs to provide, with St Martin's-in-the Fields (1722-6), an acceptable prototype for churches of the Anglican compromise.

Notes

1 See J. Simmons and H. M. Colvin, 'Staunton Harold Chapel', *Archaeological Journal*, 112 (1955), pp. 173-6.

2 For a detailed account of the building of St Columb, its many later extensions and the stylistic similarities between the cathedral and Staunton Harold, see James Stevens Curl, *The Honourable The Irish Society and the Plantation of Ulster 1608-2000* (Chichester, 2000), pp. 142-8. I am indebted to Professor Curl for the builder of Staunton Harold.

3 H. M. Colvin, 'Gothic Survival and Gothick Revival', *Architectural Review*, 103 (1948), pp. 91-8.

4 For an entirely contrary assessment of the merits of Perpendicular Gothic as a superior national building style, see John Harvey, *Henry Yevele: the Life of an English Architect* (London, 1944).

5 A claim made in the BBC Reith Lectures (broadcast weekly from 16 October to 27 November 1955): 'The Englishness of English Art'; published under the same title in an expanded and annotated version in 1964.

6 A report to the Pope from the Archpriest in 1608 assessed the number of Catholic priests active in England at that time as 'nearly 500'; see E. I. Watkin, *Roman Catholicism in England from the Reformation to 1950* (London, 1958), p. 59.

7 There was much truth in contemporary claims that the state prosecuted Catholics for treason not religion. After exhaustive study of records, Michael Questier, in his *Conversion. Politics and Religion in England 1580-1625* (Cambridge, 1996), concluded 'that the perception of an absolute, virtually institutionalised division between Protestant and Catholic concerns is misleading' (p. 204). Unfortunately Questier ignores any possible architectural manifestations of this religious flux.

8 See David Mathew, *Catholicism in England: the Portrait of a Minority*, (London, 1948), pp. 63-8. Ben Jonson converted for a time, as did Shakespeare's father and, from recent evidence from Hoghton Tower, Lancashire, so did Shakespeare himself.

9 Herefordshire Record Office, Q/RP1, Register of Papist Estates, dated 8 September 1717.

10 Adrian Morey, *The Catholic Subjects of Elizabeth I*, (Cambridge, 1978), pp. 202-15. Morey puts a persuasive case for the view that if only the Mass had been retained the majority of the population would not have been troubled by the loss of a Papal link.

11 Questier, op. cit. [note 7], pp. 45-6.

12 For Beoley, see H. M. Colvin, *Architecture and the After-Life* (New Haven and London, 1991), p. 257; figs. 222-3.

13 Morey, op. cit. [note 10], notes that in Yorkshire the proportion

of Recusant gentry had actually risen to 33% in 1603-4 from 20% in 1580-2 (p. 213).

14 During the episcopacy (1578-89) of Edmund Freke, Bishop of Norwich, Sir Thomas Cornwallis, although an open Recusant, influenced the appointment of Dr William Masters as diocesan chancellor while the Bishop's own lawyer and butler were both indicted for attending Mass; see Morey, op. cit. [note 10], p. 159. Questier, op. cit. [note 7] also supports this anecdotal evidence of doctrinal chaos.

15 For a survey of such chapels see Colvin, op. cit. [note 12], chapter 13.

16 John Newman, *The Buildings of England: West Kent and the Weald* (Harmondsworth, 1980), p. 297.

17 For the Berwick church, see John Scott, *Berwick upon Tweed: The History of the Town and Guilds* (Berwick, 1888), p. 206. See also Timothy Mowl and Brian Earnshaw, *Architecture without Kings: the Rise of Puritan Classicism under Cromwell* (Manchester, 1995), pp. 14–17.

18 For Wren or Oliver as the designer, see H. M. Colvin, 'The Church of St Mary Aldermary and its Rebuilding after the Great Fire of London', *Architectural History*, 24 (1981), pp. 24-31.

19 The Catholic orientation of Cosin's churchmanship and his consequent bias in church furnishings is indicated by his assuring a potential Catholic convert in 1628 'that the body of Christ was substantially and really in the Sacrament'; see Questier, op. cit. [note 7], p. 90.

20 There is a full account of the chapel's building history by E. W. Allfrey in *Brasenose Quatercentenary Monographs*, 3 (Oxford, 1909), pp. 18-28.

21 See R. F. Young, *Comenius in England* (Oxford, 1932).

22 J. Armitage Robinson, 'Westminster Abbey in the early part of the 17th century', *Proceedings of the Royal Institute*, 17 (1984), p. 510.

23 Garrarde to Conway, PRO: SP16, *Domestic State Papers, Charles I*, 331, no. 14.

24 See Painton Cowen, *Ancient Stained Glass in Britain*, (London, 1985), p. 118.

25 Nikolaus Pevsner, *The Buildings of England: Herefordshire* (Harmondsworth, 1963), p. 118.

26 John and Jane Penoyre, *Decorative Plasterwork in the Houses of Somerset 1500-1700* (Taunton, 1994), plates 58, 74.

27 John Collinson, *The History and Antiquities of Somerset* (London, 1791), volume 3, p. 445. Collinson was clearly confused by the evidence. He reports that Sir Edward Hext 'built also the chapel at Low Ham, where he and his Lady Dionysia lie buried under a

handsome monument of freestone ... He died Feb 22, 1634; she July 30, 1633', but adds a contradictory footnote: 'An inscription in the east window of the present chapel, says it was founded at the sole expense of George Stowel esq., May 20, anno 20 Car. ll & consecrated A.D. 1669'. George Stowel was a grandson of Sir Edward and Lady Hext. In 1669 one of the largest houses in Somerset, a virtual palace, still stood within 50 feet of Low Ham chapel, and it is worth pointing out how many of these 17th-century Gothic structures, Staunton Harold being among them, were conceived more as private chapels adjoining great houses rather than as parish churches in the ordinary sense.

28 C. W. Bracken, *A History of Plymouth and her Neighbours* (Plymouth, 1931), p. 49.

29 This Carolean star-burst tracery was destroyed in G. G. Scott's 1856 restoration. Unlike the West Country examples it was liberally encrusted with ball-flower ornament. For an illustration, see plate 227 in Gerald Cobb, *English Cathedrals. The Forgotten Centuries: Restoration and Change from 1530 to the Present Day* (London, 1980). Cobb indicates that most of the cathedrals and great churches of England suffered a gradual decay during the 17th century, exceptions being Sir Christopher Wren's repair work in the Classical style on the north-west corner of Ely's north transept (1699), and a large window with Perpendicular tracery made in the blocking wall under the tower of Bristol Cathedral in 1629.

30 Nikolaus Pevsner, *The Buildings of England: Berkshire* (Harmondsworth, 1966, reprinted 1975), p. 244, footnote citing the churchwardens' accounts, as quoted by the Rev. Basil Clarke.

31 Norman Scarfe, *Shell Guide to Suffolk* (London, 1976), p. 47, gives it to Joseph Fleming, rector 1617-36, who installed a new chancel and roof in 1633.

32 Irvine E. Gray, *The Church of St Mary the Virgin, Newent* (Newent, 1962), quotes an inscription incised in the gable at the east end of the nave above the ceiling: 'Francis Jones of Hasfield & James Hill of Cheltenham Masons were ye Head workmen in Rebuilding this Church. The first stones in ye Foundations by them were laid July 31st Anno Dom: 1675. Edward Taylor of ye Towne Carpenter was ye contriver & Head workman in Building this roofe of ye church, Anno Dom: 1679'.

33 In the discussion which followed the delivery of a version of this paper to the Georgian Group's symposium, Dr Terry Friedman suggested that the inspiration for St Mary's hall-church articulation and mandorla tracery came from St Eustache in Paris, but no evidence for this connection has yet been found.

4

Sir John Vanbrugh and the Search for a National Style

Sir John Vanbrugh and the Search for a National Style

Sir John Vanbrugh and the Search for a National Style

Giles Worsley

TO DECLARE that Sir John Vanbrugh (1664-1726) was interested in Elizabethan and earlier English architecture is not to say anything new. Over half a century ago, in 1950, Nikolaus Pevsner suggested that the plans of Seaton Delaval, Northumberland, and Vanbrugh House and Vanbrugh Castle, Greenwich, were the earliest instances of a conscious Elizabethan or Jacobean revival, or rather understanding of what that style was about.[1] In 1954 Lawrence Whistler compared photographs of the north front of Grimsthorpe Castle, Lincolnshire, with Lumley Castle, County Durham.[2] Kerry Downes developed the point in his book *Vanbrugh* (1977) and his *Sir John Vanbrugh: a Biography* (1987), citing in particular the influence of Hardwick Hall, Derbyshire, and Wollaton Hall, Nottinghamshire.[3]

But the issue has never been examined in the depth it requires. The Elizabethan elements in Vanbrugh's work are generally treated as just one feature in his architecture. They should, however, be central to our understanding of it. Nor should Vanbrugh's interest in Elizabethan architecture be seen as just one step in a steady progress towards the true Gothic Revival, with Vanbrugh caught, as one recent commentator has put it, 'on the cusp of authenticity', twinned with William Kent as a 'necessary stage towards the revival of true medieval architecture'.[4] Vanbrugh presents an alternative approach to the architecture of the past to that purveyed by the English Gothic or antiquarian movement. What interests him in his new buildings is not the detail of medieval and Tudor architecture but its form and massing, and to a lesser extent its plan. The direct imitation of specific original detail is rare. Here perhaps the comment of Vanbrugh's colleague Hawksmoor on Wollaton Hall is telling. Hawksmoor deplored the decoration 'in ye style of John Ditterlin of Strasburgh' but found that the building contained 'some true

Opposite:
The Hall, Grimsthorpe Castle, Lincolnshire (*Country Life Picture Library*).

stroaks of architecture'.[5] Presumably Vanbrugh's attitude was
much the same. This is in marked contrast to most other
English architects of the 17th and 18th centuries, for whom
it was the detail, particularly the imitation of windows, battlements and vaulting, that mattered when designing buildings that drew on England's past, not the form or massing.
His approach shows a freedom and intellectual sophistication
unexpected in a man who never trained as an architect. It is
a sophistication that finds few rivals in early-18th-century
English architecture.

Vanbrugh's use of Elizabethan models is clearest in his
skylines, both in the details and in the massing. Most of his
contemporaries preferred orderly skylines, broken perhaps by
a cupola or a calm run of Classical statues or urns. For
Vanbrugh, as for Elizabethan architects, an energetic skyline
was essential. Grouping chimneystacks was one way of
achieving this, as at King's Weston, Bristol or in the office
ranges at Blenheim Palace, Oxfordshire.[6] At Blenheim
Palace, chimneys are arranged as pairs of robust Doric
columns, a feature also found at Wollaton Hall (1580),
Burghley House, Northamptonshire (1575) and Longleat

House, Wiltshire (1572). The Elizabethan architects of those houses also pierced the skyline with obelisks, small turrets and strapwork. At Seaton Delaval and Grimsthorpe Vanbrugh achieves the same effect with altar-like urns and an emphatic balustrade silhouetted against the sky; mortar bombs topped with ducal coronets serve the same purpose on the pavilions at Blenheim. The small pyramids he placed on the lodges at Eastbury Park, Dorset, would have seemed quite appropriate to Elizabethan architects, as would the obelisks he included on the skyline of one of his unexecuted smaller house designs.[7]

Even more distinctive is the way Vanbrugh masses his buildings to create powerful silhouettes that from a distance appear like towers. The silhouette of the square pavilions rising dramatically above the roofline of Hardwick Hall (1590) finds strong echoes in Vanbrugh's first design for Eastbury Park, where the chimneystacks are grouped to give the appearance of a tower. Again it is Hardwick Hall that springs to mind when seeing the towers of the Kitchen Court at Castle Howard from across the lake. By contrast, a pair of circular drums rose at each end of Vanbrugh House (now

Eastbury Park, Dorset, first design, (from Colen Campbell, *Vitruvius Britannicus* vol. 2, (London, 1717), pl. 53).

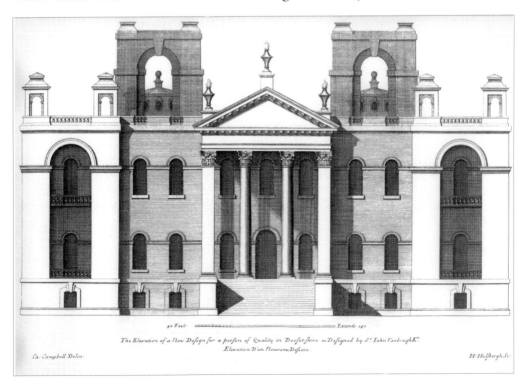

The Elevation of a New Design for a person of Quality in Dorsetshire as Designed by Sr Iohn Vanbrugh Kt.
Elevation D'un Nouveau Dessein.

Co: Campbell Delin:

H: Hulsbergh Sc:

demolished). An appropriate model could have been Robert Smythson's Worksop House, Nottinghamshire (1585).

The final design for Eastbury Park closely follows the massing of Wollaton Hall, another four-square house with tower-like corner pavilions and a clerestory rising over the

Above:
Seaton Delaval,
Northumberland
(*Country Life Picture
Library*).

centre of the house. The clerestory at Eastbury Park would have lit a great rooftop hall, an extraordinary conceit unparalleled in the work of any other architect of his day. The only apparent precedent is Wollaton Hall, which is presumably what Vanbrugh had in mind. In the event the clerestory at Eastbury Park was never completed but a comparable rooftop hall lit by clerestory windows was built at Seaton Delaval, a house that is in many ways a reduced version of Eastbury Park. At Wollaton Hall a second row of clerestory windows lights the great hall in the centre of the building. The hall at Blenheim Palace is lit by similar clerestory windows, again an unprecedented feature for the age, although one that Vanbrugh also used for the great hall at Claremont.

One of the most characteristic features of Elizabethan and Jacobean houses is the long gallery. It was a fashion that had fallen out of favour in the second half of the 17th century. Nevertheless, at Blenheim Palace Vanbrugh included a 'great gallery', a double-height room 180 feet long and between 20 and 30 feet wide, along the west side of the house.[8] In scale and impressiveness, the only fair comparison is the 166 feet long and 22-40 ft feet wide long gallery at Hardwick Hall.

In the middle of the Blenheim Palace gallery is a great semi-circular bay which reads as a bow or oriel in the centre of the west or side façade. A similar projecting bow or oriel can also be seen on the side elevation (this time on the north façade) at Burghley House, where it had originally lit the Long Gallery. The first design for Eastbury Park placed a similar bow or oriel in the centre of a principle elevation. Bows in such positions are a familiar feature of Elizabethan and Jacobean architecture: possible parallels include the entrance fronts of Campden House (*c.*1600) and Holland House (*c.*1606-7), both in Kensington and now demolished.[9] It is also possible to read the (now-destroyed) bow window at the west end of Castle Howard, which was an after-thought introduced after the Blenheim Palace bows, as an attempt to reduce the structure of such bows to a minimum, as in the bow window at Campden House.[10]

The upper level of the exterior of the Blenheim Palace bow uses caryatids to support the cornice. Vanbrugh also included caryatids in his chimneypiece in the Queen's Guard Chamber at Hampton Court, Middlesex (1716-18), and in the hall at Seaton Delaval. As Sir Howard Colvin has demonstrated, although caryatids were a common feature of Elizabethan and Jacobean houses, particularly of chimney-pieces[11] – Colvin refers to their 'indiscriminate profusion' – they had fallen entirely from fashion by the beginning of the 18th century.[12] Their use by Vanbrugh at Blenheim Palace, Hampton Court and Seaton Delaval is thus as exceptional as his inclusion of a long gallery. No doubt knowledgeable visitors would have understood the reference in both cases.

Other features characteristic of Elizabethan houses to be found in Vanbrugh's work include the idea of walled entrance courts with corner pavilions seen at Eastbury Park, Seaton Delaval and above all Grimsthorpe Castle. Syon House, Middlesex (1547-52), is a good comparison. Similarly, Vanbrugh's interest in towers, as at Claremont, Surrey, Swinstead, Lincolnshire, and the Water Tower at Kensington Palace, probably owes something to Elizabethan hunting towers. Towers were to become relatively common in 18th-

Sir John Vanbrugh and the Search for a National Style

century Gothic architecture, but this was not the case in Vanbrugh's day. Elizabethan models might include the hunting tower at Chatsworth House, Derbyshire (c.1580), which perches high on the hill above the house, much as the lodge at Claremont does.

Vanbrugh's fascination with Elizabethan and Jacobean architecture was explored most fully in his own houses, where he had no clients to worry about. Here Vanbrugh experimented more directly with Elizabethan and Jacobean plan forms. The plan of his villa at Chargate (renamed Claremont when it was sold to the Duke of Newcastle), with its central hall and wings, is clearly modelled on an Elizabethan H-plan house.[13] One could compare it, for instance, to Charlton House at Greenwich (1607-12). Vanbrugh House, built at Vanbrugh's expense for his brother Charles, followed Elizabethan tradition by having an off-centre hall and screens passage.[14] Vanbrugh Castle, which Vanbrugh built nearby for himself, shares with Holland House the idea of a circular projecting staircase tower in the centre of a main façade. Indeed, the plan of Vanbrugh Castle shares strong similarities with that of Holland House before its wings were added.

Vanbrugh Castle is a remarkable conception. It is hard to think of a contemporary comparison for this mock fort with towers and castellated fore-buildings and its now-demolished constellation of smaller buildings such as Vanbrugh House. But there is one obvious model, the Little Castle at Bolsover, Derbyshire, built for Sir Charles Cavendish from 1612. In particular, Vanbrugh may have taken the idea of narrow, projecting corner towers used at the Little Castle and applied them (without the pyramidal caps) on Vanbrugh Castle. Similar corner towers (but this time with the pyramidal caps) were proposed to be added to Sir William Sanderson's Elizabethan house in Greenwich.[15] The fore-court of Vanbrugh House with its pair of gate houses, wall, ramped entrance and projecting porch was particularly close to that of the Little Castle.

Although Vanbrugh borrowed extensively from the past he did not do so indiscriminately. In particular, he did not follow the Elizabethan fascination with large areas of

Opposite top:
Syon House,
Middlesex.

Opposite below:
Grimsthorpe Castle,
Lincolnshire.

(Both from *Country Life Picture Library*).

Vanbrugh Castle, Greenwich, drawn by William Stukeley, 1721 *(Society of Antiquaries).*

glazing (the bow window at the west end of Castle Howard is the one possible exception). Instead, he argued against large windows, preferring to retain a low ratio of window to wall, and used round-headed windows, for which there is no Elizabethan or Jacobean precedent. Nor did he imitate the Elizabethan fashion for a highly decorated façade and profusion of orders evident at Wollaton. As he explained to the Earl of Manchester: 'tis certainly the Figure and Proportions that make the most pleasing Fabrick, And not the delicacy of the Ornaments.'[16]

Such a wealth of reference to Elizabethan and Jacobean buildings is exceptional in English architecture of this date, or indeed of any date in the second half of the 17th or the 18th centuries. Nor is there any reason to believe that the architecture-obsessed Vanbrugh would not have known these earlier houses. They were after all among the greatest buildings of an age that clearly fascinated him, were owned by leading aristocrats, many of them his friends or clients, and were all easily accessible. Most of them lay around London or were within a day's ride of each other in the north Midlands. Burghley House, owned by the Earl of Exeter, lay just off the Great North Road outside Stamford, where Vanbrugh would have regularly broken his journey on the way north to Castle Howard. Wollaton Hall lies on the outskirts of Nottingham, the principal city in the region, where many key roads crossed and a city in which one of Vanbrugh's most persistent clients, the Duke of Newcastle, was a major figure. The Duke of Newcastle also owned Bolsover Castle, which lay about five miles from his principal seat, Welbeck Abbey, where Vanbrugh set out the lake in 1703 and made designs for a new house.[17] Worksop Manor, owned by the Duke of Norfolk, lay on the neighbouring estate. Hardwick Hall, four miles to the south of Bolsover, was owned by the Duke of Devonshire, with whom Vanbrugh stayed for four or five days in 1699 at Chatsworth House, itself only 14 miles away.

The critical event in Vanbrugh's architectural education was probably the tour he made in the summer of 1699, the

The Little Castle, Bolsover, Derbyshire (*Country Life Picture Library*).

year he first turned to architecture. As he explained to the Earl of Manchester on Christmas Day that year: 'I have been this Summer at my Ld Carlisle's, and Seen most of the great houses in the North, as Ld Nottings: Duke of Leeds Chattesworth &c.'[18] When set beside that sweeping statement – 'most of the great houses in the North' – the list of houses is frustratingly short – Vanbrugh only mentions houses where building work was then going on – but it suggests an itinerary that would have taken him past the doors of all the key houses. The Earl of Nottingham's house was Burley-on-the-Hill in Rutland. Assuming that Vanbrugh was coming from London he would have just passed Burghley House when he turned off the Great North Road at Stamford for Burley-on the-Hill, which lay 10 miles to the west. From Burley-on-the-Hill the obvious way to Chatsworth House would have been through Melton Mowbray and Nottingham, past Wollaton Hall. From Nottingham the road goes to Mansfield and then passes between Hardwick Hall and Bolsover before arriving at Chesterfield and so on to Chatsworth House. From Chatsworth House he would have been unlikely to have missed Welbeck Abbey and Worksop House as he headed north for Kiveton Hall, which lies seven miles away.

So what was Vanbrugh trying to achieve in this self-conscious and highly original series of references back to an earlier English architecture? Understanding Vanbrugh's aesthetic motivation is not easy as he left few clues to his thinking and no record of his library. One piece of evidence is his well-known letter of 1707 to the Earl of Manchester, for whom Vanbrugh remodelled Kimbolton Castle, Huntingdonshire:

> As to the Outside, I thought 'twas absolutely best, to give it Something of the Castle Air, tho' at the Same time to make it regular ... This method was practic'd at Windsor in King Charles's time, And has been universally Approv'd ... to have built a Front with Pillasters, and what the Orders require cou'd never have been born with the Rest of the Castle: I'm sure this will make a very Noble and Masculine Shew; and is of as Warrantable a kind of building as Any.'[19]

It is easy to assume that this letter provides the key to explaining Vanbrugh's architectural approach – easy but dangerous. Vanbrugh was not writing to Lord Manchester about the design of a new house but about an ancient house that was to be remodelled. Hence his concern about what could 'be born with the Rest of the Castle'.

This search for a 'Castle Air', of worrying about designing in sympathy with existing fabric, was an essentially antiquarian idea which was surprisingly prevalent in the late 17th and early 18th centuries.[20] It could be found in country houses, such as Drayton House, Northamptonshire, where a new castellated gate range with a central tower was added in the 1660s and 1670s; universities, where Vanbrugh may have known Tom Tower at Christ Church, Oxford, of 1681; and churches, as in Wren and Hawksmoor's work at Westminster Abbey. It was into this strong tradition that Vanbrugh's work at Kimbolton Castle and Lumley Castle fits. In both cases, Vanbrugh was essentially concerned with decorative features – hence his consequent use of crenellations at both Kimbolton Castle and Lumley Castle, features that he otherwise used only at Vanbrugh Castle – not with form and massing. The similarity between Kimbolton and Drayton House, with its sham fortifications, would have been even greater had Vanbrugh persuaded the Earl of Manchester to accept his plea to replace the outbuildings with a series of towers round a perimeter wall, which would have given the house the impression of a castle with keep and curtain wall.[21] The model here is probably a building he knew well, the Château de Vincennes outside Paris, where Vanbrugh was incarcerated, although the immediate source was probably Jacques Androuet du Cerceau's plan of Vincennes in *Les Plus Excellents Bastiments de France*.[22]

Vanbrugh's proposed addition to Sir William Sanderson's house at Greenwich of slim towers modelled on those of the Little Castle at Bolsover also fits in with his interest in the 'Castle Air'.[23] It is in this context that one should also look at any new work carried out by Vanbrugh at Audley End, Essex.[24]

But Vanbrugh's work at Kimbolton Castle, Lumley Castle, Sir William Sanderson's house and Audley End

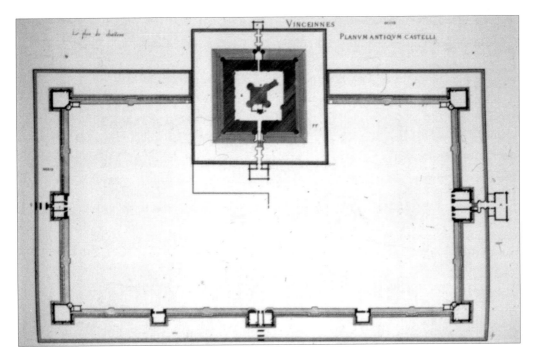

Above:
Plan of Château de
Vincennes (from
Jacques Androuet du
Cerceau's *Les Plus
Excellents Bastiments de
France* (fascimile, Paris
1988), p. 44).

Below:
Sir John Vanbrugh,
plan of Kimbolton
Castle,
Huntingdonshire
(from Lawrence
Whistler, *The
Imagination of Sir John
Vanbrugh* (London,
1954), fig. 48).

involved alterations to existing buildings. His contemporaries, such as Wren and Hawksmoor, had no doubts that when it came to designing new buildings the Classical language was the only appropriate one to use. Where Vanbrugh

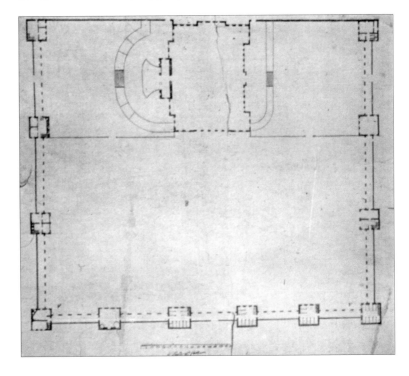

is exceptional is that he used historical models for his new buildings. This cannot be explained away by an antiquarian interest in the 'Castle Air'.

When designing new buildings Vanbrugh was using the past to invigorate architectural design. He was not concerned with the careful use of the symbols of antiquity, such as crenellations, but with abstracting the essence of Elizabethan and Jacobean buildings. More specifically, it would seem that he was making a deliberate attempt to create not an architecture mired in the past but a new and yet self-consciously English architecture, a 'National Style'.

The England of Vanbrugh's day was an increasingly self-confident nation. After the disastrous 17th century, when England had been torn apart by the Civil War, invaded by the Scots, beaten repeatedly by the Dutch at sea and finally invaded again by a Dutch army which overthrew the English king, the years of the Duke of Marlborough's triumphant campaigns were a liberation. With such victories as Blenheim, Malplaquet and Oudenaarde and the signing of the Treaty of Utrecht in 1713 the English could hold their heads up high. It was natural that this confident mood should be represented in architecture. Indeed, it is probably fair to see Blenheim Palace and Vanbrugh's National Style as continuing the struggle on a cultural front.

For an English architect casting round for a model on which to build a National Style the country houses of the reigns of Queen Elizabeth and James I would have been an obvious place to start. The architecture of the two generations immediately preceding Vanbrugh had been one of deliberate restraint. What might be termed the Pratt-May model of the country house introduced at Kingston Lacy, Dorset, and Eltham Lodge, Kent - a simple, Palladian, generally astylar, tripartite pedimented house - became commonplace.

When Vanbrugh cast around for a more inspiring model for the great national monument that was to be Blenheim Palace it was hardly surprising that he should look beyond such houses to Elizabethan and Jacobean prodigy houses, for Blenheim Palace is by any standards a prodigy house. These houses exuded confidence, outstripping

Opposite above:
Grimsthorpe Castle,
Lincolnshire.

Opposite below:
Lumley Castle,
County Durham.

(*Country Life Picture
Library*).

anything built later for scale and architectural ambition. What was more, the years of Elizabeth's reign were implanted in the English consciousness as years of greatness. The defeat of the Spanish Armada ranked alongside the Battle of Blenheim in the scale of its triumph. And, one should not forget, as Mark Girouard suggests, that as a playwright intimately involved in a theatrical world where the works of Shakespeare and Fletcher were still regularly performed, Vanbrugh may have felt a special affinity to Elizabethan architecture.[25]

There was, also, a particular appropriateness in using Elizabethan architecture as a model for Blenheim Palace. The great Elizabethan houses - Hatfield House, Hertfordshire, Theobalds Palace, Hertfordshire, Burghley House - were all built as palaces for a queen who did not occupy them. It was thus vicariously that a female monarch could express herself through architectural magnificence. The same was true of Blenheim Palace, built by a royal favourite for another female monarch, Queen Anne. As Vanbrugh wrote to the Duchess of Marlborough: 'Tho' ordered to be a Dwelling house for the Duke of Marlborough and his posterity at the Same time by all the World esteemed and looked on as a Publick Edifice, raised for a Monument of the Queen's Glory through his great Genius.'[26] The point was made to Lord Harley the same year in a sentiment that Lord Burghley would have recognised when Vanbrugh stated that he looked 'upon it [Blenheim Palace] much more as an intended Monument to the Queen's Glory than a private Habitation for the Duke'.[27]

One should be careful not to take the Elizabethan analogy too far. There are also strong medieval overtones in Vanbrugh's work. The great square corner towers rising massive and dominant over Grimsthorpe Castle echo the late-medieval quadrilateral castles or fortified homes of the north, such as Bolton Castle and Wressle Castle in Yorkshire, and particularly Lumley Castle, where Vanbrugh worked. Similarly the East Gate at Blenheim Palace, with its massive round-headed archway, is perhaps best seen as Vanbrugh's reinterpretation of Norman city or castle gates, such as Micklegate Bar in York.

The machicolations which Vanbrugh used on the gateway at Eastbury Park, the towers at Claremont, the

brewhouse at Kings Weston, the Pyramid Gate at Castle Howard and extensively on Vanbrugh Castle have obvious late-medieval rather than Elizabethan associations. One thinks, perhaps, of Bodiam and Herstmonceux Castles in Sussex, Tattershall Castle in Lincolnshire or Chipchase Castle in Northumberland. The intended association is specifically military. The same is true of the round windows suggesting portholes or cannonholes that sprout across Blenheim Palace, in the basement and quadrants of the north front, in the central range and pavilions of the south front, and, fittingly, flanking the East Gate. Such a motif is most appropriate for a great military commander and Master of the Ordnance. They also appeared at Eastbury Park (where in one design Vanbrugh even considered including them in the attic of the main building), Claremont and Lumley Castle.

Just as it was the essence of Elizabethan and Jacobean architecture that Vanbrugh abstracted, not its detail, so the same is true of medieval buildings. Here one needs to look carefully at Vanbrugh's architectural language. The extensive use of the orders gives it a Classical air, but the particular choice of Classical vocabulary - the giant order, particularly Doric and Corinthian, round-headed and circular windows, arcading and giant keystones - is telling. This is not conventional Classicism. Vanbrugh uses the giant order repeatedly. At Blenheim Palace, for instance, it appears framing the gateways to the kitchen and stable court towers, in the portico and flanking bays of the entrance front, in the hall (on two different scales), and on the garden front. At Seaton Delaval it is found on both entrance and garden fronts. Eastbury Park had a giant portico of Doric columns. At Grimsthorpe Castle, as at Seaton Delaval, pairs of columns flank the entrance.

In each case, except on the portico of the garden front at Seaton Delaval, Vanbrugh uses the Corinthian or Doric orders. The Ionic order, by contrast, is reserved for occasions where Vanbrugh is being most self-evidently Classical, for pedimented porticos on the north front at Stowe, on the Temple of the Winds at Castle Howard and on the Bagnio at Eastbury. Vanbrugh's version of the Doric order is also unusual in its horizontal grooving. Palladio's Villa Sarego, as

The Hall, Blenheim
Palace, Oxfordshire
(*Country Life Picture
Library*).

illustrated in the *Quattro Libri*,[28] could be a precedent for this
but the Villa Sarego order is Ionic. Other sources could be
Sanmicheli's Porta Palio in Verona (although it is unclear
whether Vanbrugh could have known of it), Sansovino's
Zecca or Mint in Venice, which was well illustrated in
engravings, or Androuet du Cerceau's Château de
Charleval.[29] Probably Vanbrugh's source was Serlio's Tuscan
order, as suggested for city and fortress gates,[30] giving it a
particularly forceful, masculine, or – and this is what is probably important – almost primitive feel.

It is important to remember how innovative Vanbrugh
was in using the giant order. Before Vanbrugh and
Hawksmoor took it up at the turn of the 17th century at
Greenwich Hospital, Easton Neston and Castle Howard the
giant order was rare in English architecture.[31] The use
Vanbrugh put it to was also often highly original. In the hall
at Blenheim Palace and in the pairs of columns on the
entrance fronts of Seaton Delaval and Grimsthorpe Castle
and on either side of the archways at Blenheim Palace he

makes no attempt to use the giant order in its traditional, quasi-structural role. Instead he seems to display it almost as a symbol.

Vanbrugh's interest in the giant order is unlikely to come from Elizabethan architecture. Although used at Kirby Hall, Northamptonshire, and at Hill Hall, Essex, the giant order is rare in Elizabethan or Jacobean architecture. But it was a distinctive feature of Romanesque and Gothic architecture. One only has to think of Gloucester or Salisbury cathedrals to appreciate its importance in the Middle Ages. Is it coincidence that the two giant orders Vanbrugh uses most consistently are the Doric and the Corinthian, both of which (if we set aside post-Renaissance preconceptions of what the orders should look like) are readily identifiable in medieval architecture? Gloucester and Salisbury, for instance, can both be read as forms of Doric; the choir of Canterbury Cathedral of 1174 or the hall of Oakham Castle of the 1180s are obviously Corinthian. Could Vanbrugh's symbolic use of the giant Doric and Corinthian orders have been meant to generate associations with their use in medieval buildings?

Below:
The Hall,
Oakham Castle,
Rutland.

Opposite:
The Hall,
Grimsthorpe Castle,
Lincolnshire.

(*Country Life Picture Library*).

Sir John Vanbrugh and the Search for a National Style

It could be argued that the giant order is too common a feature of early-18th-century architecture for Vanbrugh's use of it on its own to present a convincing argument about his relationship with medieval architecture. But Vanbrugh also made repeated use of the round-headed window, often in combination with the giant order.[32] Castle Howard, Blenheim Palace, Claremont and Grimsthorpe Castle all are, or were, dominated by round-headed windows, and the same is true of many of Vanbrugh's smaller buildings, such as the brewhouse at King's Weston and the belvedere at Claremont. Round-headed windows are otherwise hard to find in English domestic architecture of the late 17th or early 18th centuries, but there is an obvious precedent with which we know Vanbrugh was familiar, Hugh May's remodelling of Windsor Castle. This suggests that for Vanbrugh there was a clear association between round-headed windows and medieval architecture, as a glance at the Tower of London would have confirmed.[33]

Vanbrugh's use of arcading - which can be found along

the flanking wings at Claremont, in the kitchen court at Blenheim Palace and the base courts at Seaton Delaval, Eastbury Park and Grimsthorpe Castle, and very powerfully, in the superimposed arcades of the halls at Blenheim Palace, Seaton Delaval and Grimsthorpe Castle - also has medieval overtones. The impression given by these halls is almost that of sitting within the double-height hall of a Norman keep - one thinks of the keep of Rochester Castle, Kent. This is unlikely to be coincidence. The round-headed arch is the most powerful motif of early-medieval architecture. Superimposed arcades are a characteristic feature of Romanesque cathedrals, such as Durham.

The sense of primitive, medieval associations grows

North-east transept, Salisbury Cathedral, Wiltshire (*English Heritage, National Monuments Record*, A42/5004, photographed 1942).

Sir John Vanbrugh and the Search for a National Style

stronger in Vanbrugh's later buildings as he drops the mouldings that relieve the round-headed windows at Castle
Howard and the arcading of the hall at Blenheim Palace and
Seaton Delaval and replaces them with heavy, unrelieved
impost blocks. These can be seen in the wings added at
Claremont from 1715, in the first design for Eastbury Park
(1716), Vanbrugh Castle (1718) and, above all, at Grimsthorpe
Castle (1722). Here the arcading of the north elevation and
particularly the hall attains a primitive quality that makes the
hall at Blenheim Palace seem almost refined.

It might also be asked whether Vanbrugh's use of the
tripartite Serlian window, with its heightened central light,
apparently the most 'Palladian' of his architectural motifs, had
medieval connotations for him.[34] Three-light windows with
a raised central light are an important feature of Early English
cathedrals, such as Worcester, Lincoln, Ripon and, most evidently, Salisbury.

With Elizabethan and Jacobean form and massing, and
medieval architectural elements, what Vanbrugh seems to be
trying to do is to abstract the essence of the most impressive
features of English architecture, while retaining a language
that remains recognisably Classical, to create a National Style.

Vanbrugh was not alone in this approach to architectural language, although he was the most consistent architect
to use it in England. Many Baroque churches, particularly in
Germany, retained the twin towers of the west front that had

Side elevation of first
proposed design for
Eastbury, Dorset (from
Colen Campbell,
Vitruvius Britannicus
vol. 2 (London, 1717),
pl. 55.)

been established as the classic form for grand ecclesiastical architecture in Romanesque. Sir Christopher Wren's City of London church spires reinterpreted the medieval concept of the tall, thin spire with a Classical vocabulary.

In France, the idea that Classical detail could be married with traditional forms and massing had been established since the Renaissance, most famously at François I's Château de Chambord. Mark Girouard has highlighted the way that medieval towers were often retained when French châteaux were rebuilt, whether in the 16th century, as at the Château de la Tour d'Aigues, or in the 18th century, as at the Château de Missery. Elsewhere, as at the Château de Chambord, medieval massing was combined with the new Classical language. Jacques de Daillon and his son Jean, for example, who had experienced the new Renaissance style at first hand during the Italian wars under Louis XII and François I, mixed the form of a medieval castle - great circular towers, a drawbridge and formidable machicolations - with large windows and fashionable Classical detail when they rebuilt the Château de le Lude.[35]

A parallel can also be found in the way French architects looked at Gothic churches. In England, apart from Wren, there was little interest in the structural possibilities of Gothic architecture until the 19th century.[36] Instead English architects extrapolated Gothic detail with increasing accuracy for application to structures that were essentially Classical in form. In France it was the reverse. Architects were fascinated by the structural possibility of Gothic churches but were happy to give the churches they built Classical detail.

Similar parallels could be found elsewhere. Southern German and Swiss Baroque churches, such as St Florian, with repetitive east and west fronts may have been harking back to Ottonian churches. In Portugal, Nicolò Nasoni's tower of the Clerigos in Oporto, which rises to a height of 250 feet, has been compared to the medieval tower of the Palazzo Communale in his native Siena.[37] Close examination would probably reveal other examples.

The most interesting comparison with Vanbrugh is his close contemporary Johann Santini Aichel (1677–1723), who trained as a painter and then turned to architecture, combining Gothic and Classical forms in a remarkable series of churches and buildings in Bohemia from 1702. As with Vanbrugh, there was an overtly political, indeed triumphalist, context to his work. In Vanbrugh's case it was the military success of Protestant England, in Santini's, the counter-Reformationary re-establishment of Roman Catholicism in Bohemia after the suppression of Protestantism. His first work was the rebuilding of the Cistercian abbey church of Sedlec, which had been burnt by the Hussites in 1421. As in the case of Vanbrugh it was a *tour de force* for which Santini seems to have had no training, although he did come from a family of masons.

In England, Vanbrugh's work appears exceptional, but a number of buildings seem to reveal the influence of his thinking. The Debtors' Prison in York Castle of 1709 is articulated by a giant Doric order whose centrepiece is formed by pairs of giant Doric pilasters, horizontally grooved as in Vanbrugh's buildings. At Compton Verney, which was rebuilt around 1714 deliberately retaining the medieval plan of courtyard and great hall, the south front with its giant Doric order and round-headed windows was probably meant to read as a medievalising elevation.[38] Biddenden House, Wiltshire, built in 1711 for one of Marlborough's generals, John Webb (who retired from active service after a wound at Malplaquet and was appointed Commander-in-Chief of the Home Forces in 1712), again has round-headed windows. It also has castellations, a tower and prominent displays of armour above the frontispiece.[39]

In each case, an association with history or military traditions (the site in York Castle, the long-established Verney family, the martial identity of General Webb) would have made Vanbrugh's National Style appropriate. This suggests a plausible rationale for the powerful group of buildings erected by the Board of Ordnance between 1715 and 1724, particularly the old Board of Ordnance and Grand Square at Woolwich Arsenal, Devonport Gun Wharf, the barracks at Berwick upon Tweed and the gateway and Great Storehouse at Chatham Dockyard.

Vanbrugh had close connections with the key figures at the Board of Ordnance. The Duke of Marlborough, his

Sir John Vanbrugh and the Search for a National Style

patron at Blenheim Palace, was Master of the Ordnance; the Surveyor-General, Brigadier Richards, was a friend.[40] But the exact responsibility for these buildings remains obscure, although Richard Hewlings's discovery that Hawksmoor designed the barracks at Berwick suggests that he may have been responsible. But whoever's hand held the pencil, the architectural language and logic were the same that Vanbrugh displayed in his houses, reduced to an austere severity fitting the buildings' purpose. The vocabulary is the same, the towers, the machicolations, the round-headed and circular windows (the latter particularly appropriate for the Board of Ordnance). Looking at the gateway at Chatham and at the impressive length of the Great Storehouse with its four towers silhouetted against the skyline it is clear that we are supposed to read what we see as castles. Indeed, the Great Storehouse with its four towers and round-headed windows could well be seen as a reinterpretation of the similarly four-towered, round-windowed, east front of Windsor Castle, the *locus classicus* for Vanbrugh of his National Style.

These buildings are the physical representation on land of the material strength of the Royal Navy, on which English security rested. Where Blenheim Palace celebrated military victory, these buildings are the foundations of future naval victories. What more appropriate language could there be for them than Vanbrugh's National Style?

And what about a building such as John James's Little Stanmore church, Middlesex, of 1714-15 where a new nave was added to an existing medieval tower? Was the choice of austere round-headed windows and the giant order a deliberate medieval evocation? When we see a pointed arched window we know to call it Gothic. We do so because studies of the Gothic or antiquarian movement are based on the assumption that it leads to the Gothic Revival in the 19th century and we thus spend our time looking for clues that point towards it. Perhaps we should display a similar sensitivity to the use of round-headed windows. We should certainly cease to examine the Gothic or antiquarian movement through the prism of mid-19th-century assumptions about medieval architecture.

Is there a theoretical foundation to Vanbrugh's

Opposite above:
The Great Storehouse, Chatham Dockyard, Kent.

Opposite below:
The Gateway, Chatham Dockyard. (*Country Life Picture Library*).

approach? In his article 'Seeing Vanbrugh and Hawksmoor'[41] David Cast picked out a key phrase which Hawksmoor used when describing Vanbrugh's designs for a belvedere at Castle Howard. 'What Sir John proposes,' he wrote, 'is well and founded upon ye Rules of ye Ancients. I mean by that upon Strong Reason and Good Fancy, joyn'd with Experience and Tryalls.' Cast goes on to discuss the use of the word Fancy.[42] 'Fancy, as understood in England, was something close to Imagination, the part of the mind that envisages Ideas and Images, elements that come more from the mind itself than from nature, that is to say, less from mimesis, the imitation of the natural world, than from the separate world of intelligence.'[43]

Cast argues that Hawksmoor was alluding to Thomas Hobbes: 'if we come across phrases like "the quickening pulse" or "unexpected curiosity", or see an idea like Hawksmoor's "Good Fancy" we are entirely justified in tracing these back to the writings of Hobbes'. As he explains, 'Hobbes knew of Judgement, but his essential materialism, which directed him to politics, made him in time think of art not as ideal imitation but as mere resemblance and, as such, based on Fancy.'[44]

Was it this Hobbesian concept of 'Fancy' which allowed Vanbrugh to break with the Classical conventions and create a new architecture which combined earlier form with Classical detail? Fancy might also help explain why Vanbrugh's approach never caught on. For the 3rd Earl of Shaftesbury, true architecture was 'independent of Fancy'.

A more directly architectural influence may have been the thinking of Claude Perrault, one of the most controversial architectural theorists of the time. Vanbrugh was certainly aware of Perrault's work. He subscribed to John James's translation of the *Treatise of the Five Orders* in 1707 and it is likely that Perrault's edition of Vitruvius, published in 1684, was a source for some of Vanbrugh's garden buildings.[45] Lee Morrissey argues that Vanbrugh's position in England had parallels with Perrault's argument with French Classicism. In particular, Perrault undermined the mathematical, universal understanding of Vitruvian architectural theory, pointing out that if music is to be considered as an analogy for architecture it is important to take into account the cultural differences in music. The way 'harmonies' are applied 'differs with different musicians and countries, just as the application of architectural proportions differs with different authors and buildings'.[46] This suggested that instead of there being one, universal Classicism which architects had to follow it was valid for different nationalities to develop their own form of Classicism, an argument that for Vanbrugh could have been a justification for his attempt to form an English style.

There is also one further possible source that needs examining, Jacques Androuet du Cerceau's *Les Plus Excellents Bastiments de France*. Published in two volumes in 1576 and 1579, Du Cerceau's book is filled with detailed engravings of French châteaux by a variety of architects, including Du Cerceau, caught on the cusp between the Gothic of the Middle Ages and Classicism of the Renaissance. Some of the châteaux shown, such as Montargis, are almost entirely medieval and Gothic. Others, such as Serlio's Ancy-le-Franc or the Tuileries, are determinedly up-to-date in their Classicism. Many combine both in a way that is often surprisingly similar to Vanbrugh's work.

Du Cerceau has seldom been given much attention by British architectural historians, although he is acknowledged as a source for 16th-century builders.[47] Instead, the focus has generally been on the more conventionally Classical works published in Italy, Vignola's *Regole delle Cinque Ordini* of 1562, Serlio's *L'Architettura*, published in various books between 1537 and 1551 and above all Palladio's *Quattro Libri* of 1570. But Du Cerceau's book, with its large and clear engravings, would have made a very attractive sourcebook. As no record of Vanbrugh's library survives we do not know whether he owned a copy, but Wren and Hawksmoor did.[48]

The possibility that Du Cerceau's plan of the Château de Vincennes could have been the model for Vanbrugh's proposed castle-like outbuildings at Kimbolton Castle has already been discussed. Vanbrugh's plan of Seaton Delaval set within its bastions also bears striking similarities to the plan of Château de Chambord.[49] Circular windows, which are an important feature of Vanburgh's work, are not common in

Château de
Charleval (from
Jacques Androuet
du Cerceau's *Les
Plus Excellents
Bastiments de France*,
(fascimile, Paris
1988), p. 212).

English architecture but they can be found elsewhere in Du
Cerceau - at Verneul, Chantilly, Dampierre, Challuau and
Charleval - just as round-headed windows are also found, at
La Muette, Blois, Challuau and Charleval.

It is the Château de Charleval, which Du Cerceau
designed, that provides the closest parallels between Vanbrugh
and Du Cerceau.[50] It is remarkable how many of the elements used at Charleval are also found in Vanbrugh's limited
palette: the grooved rustication of the Doric columns, the
round-headed and circular windows, emphatic keystones,
even caryatids.

Other parallels between Du Cerceau and Vanbrugh include the unusual pedimentless portico at Escouam, which recalls that at Seaton Delaval;[51] the high-level caryatids supporting the frontispiece at Escouam, which could have helped justify the use of caryatids in the bow window at Blenheim Palace;[52] the pyramided lodges at Saint Germain that are reminiscent of those at Eastbury Park[53] and the strange lanterns on the east and west wings at Blenheim Palace that may owe something to the lantern at Blois as illustrated by Du Cerceau.[54]

Du Cerceau could have appealed to Vanbrugh as a model that showed how he could break the stranglehold of Classical rules and assumptions epitomised by Palladio's *Quattro Libri*. He would have been aware that the buildings illustrated were contemporaries of the Elizabethan buildings that so impressed him in England, with which they not only share many characteristics but for which they are often the sources. Above all, the buildings illustrated show how Classical and traditional architectural models could be combined to produce an architecture that was both rooted in national history and yet up-to-date.

Vanbrugh's vision of a self-consciously English architecture was not to be. His challenge to the canons of Classical architecture was too radical to be accepted. By his death in 1726 the architectural freedom of the first two decades of the century had been replaced by neo-Palladian hegemony. In these circumstances Vanbrugh's architectural language proved shortlived and his National Style died with him, but not before creating some of the most remarkable buildings ever erected in England.[55]

Notes
1 Nikolaus Pevsner, 'Good King James Gothic', *Architectural Review*, 107 (1950), p. 117. Pevsner considered only the outlines of these houses. He did not note that the plan of Seaton Delaval, like that of Eastbury, is based on Palladio's Villa Poiana: see Giles Worsley, *Classical Architecture in Britain: the Heroic Age* (New Haven and London, 1995), p. 93.
2 Lawrence Whistler, *The Imagination of Sir John Vanbrugh* (London, 1954), p. 17, figs 130-1.
3 Kerry Downes, *Vanbrugh* (London, 1977), pp. 50-4, 69, 104, 116;

Kerry Downes, *Sir John Vanbrugh: a Biography* (London, 1987), pp. 290, 331-51, 455, 459. Downes also noted the Elizabethan origins of the east and west windows at Blenheim (without giving any source), of the clerestories at Blenheim and Seaton Delaval and of the plan and elevation of Chargate. See also Mark Girouard, 'Attitudes to Elizabethan Architecture 1600-1900', in Sir John Summerson (editor), *Concerning Architecture* (London, 1968), pp. 14-15.

4 Timothy Mowl, 'Antiquaries, Theatre and Early Medievalism', in Christopher Ridgway and Robert Williams (editors), *Sir John Vanbrugh and Landscape Architecture in Baroque England 1690-1730* (Stroud, 2000), pp. 91, 92.

5 Mark Girouard, op. cit. [note 3], p. 14.

6 It is important to remember that at Blenheim Vanbrugh was working in association with Hawksmoor. One cannot therefore be certain to which man individual details can be ascribed.

7 Geoffrey Beard, *The Work of John Vanbrugh*, (London, 1986), fig. 96.

8 There were also practical reasons for a gallery on this scale, given the size of some of the paintings presented by grateful cities in the Netherlands to the Duke of Marlborough.

9 Other examples might include Thornbury Castle in Gloucestershire (*c.*1515-20), Hengrave Hall, Suffolk (*c.*1525-38), Hartwell House, Buckinghamshire, Fountains Hall, Yorkshire, the Hall at Bradford-on-Avon, Wiltshire (*c.*1600), Crewe Hall, Cheshire.

10 Lawrence Whistler, op. cit. [note 2], pl. 8.

11 Howard Colvin, *Essays in English Architectural History* (New Haven and London, 1999), pp. 95-126.

12 A rare exception is the pair of caryatids supporting the frontispiece of William Talman's hall range at Drayton House, Northamptonshire, of 1702.

13 Downes suggests that the unusual H-plan may be the result of Vanbrugh building on the foundations of an earlier Elizabethan farmhouse. This seems unlikely. Houses built using earlier foundations usually adapted them to contemporary fashion.

14 Kerry Downes, *Vanbrugh*, op. cit. [note 3], fig. 13a.

15 H. M. Colvin and Maurice Craig, *Architectural Drawings in the Library of Elton Hall by Sir John Vanbrugh and Sir Edward Lovett Pearce* (Roxburghe Club, 1964), XLa.

16 Lawrence Whistler, op. cit. [note 2], p. 15.

17 Kerry Downes, *Vanbrugh*, op. cit. [note 3], p. 461.

18 Ibid., p. 26.

19 Ibid., p. 48.

20 Giles Worsley, *Classical Architecture in Britain: the Heroic Age* (New Haven and London, 1995), pp. 179–88.

21 Lawrence Whistler, op. cit. [note 2], fig. 48.

22 Jacques Androuet du Cerceau, *Les Plus Excellents Bastiments de France*, edited by David Thomson (Paris, 1988), p. 212.

23 H. M. Colvin and Maurice Craig, op. cit. [note 15], Xla. Sanderson's house has been demolished and its site is occupied by Greenwich Hospital.

24 The suggestion that the Jacobean-Revival screen at Audley End, Essex, was designed by Vanbrugh (Nikolaus Pevsner, op. cit. [note 1], 117) is doubted by Paul Drury, '"No other palace in the Kingdom will compare with it": the Evolution of Audley End', *Architectural History*, 23 (1980), pp. 27–9.

25 Mark Girouard, op. cit. [note 3], p. 15. See also Kerry Downes, *Vanbrugh*, op. cit. [note 3], pp. 50–4.

26 Lawrence Whistler, op. cit. [note 2], p. 237.

27 Kerry Downes, *Vanbrugh*, op. cit. [note 3], p. 58.

28 Andrea Palladio, *I Quattro Libri dell' Architettura* (Venice, 1570), volume 2, p. 67.

29 Jacques Androuet du Cerceau, op. cit. [note 22], pp. 212–13.

30 Sebastiano Serlio, *On Architecture* (New Haven and London, 1996), p. 260.

31 In the middle of the 17th century the giant order can be found at Lees Court, Kent, and Bayhall, Kent, in the 1650s and at Greenwich Palace, Eltham Lodge, Kent, and Cornbury Park, Oxfordshire, in the 1660s. Thereafter it is unusual, although it appears on the south front of Chatsworth House, Derbyshire, in 1687, where its use is probably derived from Greenwich Palace, and in the pedimented frontispiece at Kiveton House, Yorkshire in 1694. A handful of examples of its use can be found at the beginning of the 18th century - at Addiscombe House, Surrey (1702–3), Cound Hall, Shropshire (1704), Herriard Park, Hampshire (1704), Wotton House, Buckinghamshire (1704), and Buckingham House in London (1705) - all of which can probably be traced to Wren, Hawksmoor and Vanbrugh's work at Greenwich Palace.

32 The combination appears fully formed on the entrance elevation of Vanbrugh's first building, Castle Howard.

33 Vanbrugh would also have been aware that Jules-Hardouin Mansart used round-headed windows on the main and ground floors of Versailles.

34 On the extension of Vanbrugh Castle, the towers of Seaton Delaval, Grimsthorpe Castle and in designs for Eastbury Park.

35 Mark Girouard, *Life in the French Country House* (London, 2000), pp. 77–8.

36 One thinks particularly of St Paul's Cathedral and St Dunstan-in-the-East.

37 Anthony Blunt (editor), *Baroque and Rococo Architecture and Decoration* (Ware, 1978), p. 321.

38 This is surely a paraphrase of the north front of Castle Howard, although Stephen Brindle cautions citing the niche in the ground-floor bays between the pilasters as a comparison with similar niches at Castle Howard. These are shown open in Robert Adam's plan of the house of 1760 (Stephen Brindle, 'Compton Verney: an Architectural History of the House', in Robert Bearman (editor), *Compton Verney: a History of the House and its Owners* (Stratford-upon-Avon, 2000), pp. 105-8, pl. 21), although in Adam's engraving of the plan these windows are closed (op. cit., pl. 27).

39 Quendon Hall, Essex, is another possible example that would be worth examining: John Kenworthy-Browne et al., *Burke's and Savill's Guide to Country Houses, III, East Anglia* (London, 1981), pp. 68-9.

40 Lawrence Whistler, op. cit. [note 2], pp. 212-14,

41 David Cast, 'Seeing Vanbrugh and Hawksmoor', *Journal of the Society of Architectural Historians*, 43 (December, 1984), pp. 310-27.

42 Quoted in Cast, op. cit. [note 41], p. 315.

43 Ibid.

44 Ibid., p. 316.

45 Giles Worsley, '"After ye Antique": Vanbrugh, Hawksmoor and Kent', in Ridgway and Williams, op. cit [note 4], pp. 137, 147.

46 Lee Morrissey, *From the Temple to the Castle* (Charlottesville and London, 1999), p. 59.

47 John Summerson, *Architecture in Britain 1530-1830* (London, 1977), 56; Nicholas Cooper, *Houses of the Gentry 1480-1680* (New Haven and London, 1999), p. 169.

48 David Watkin (editor), *Sale Catalogues of Eminent Persons, Volume 4: Architects* (London, 1972), pp. 37, 105.

49 Du Cerceau, op. cit. [note 22], p. 48; Robert Williams, 'Fortified Gardens', fig. 36, in Ridgway and Williams, op. cit. [note 4], pp. 137, 147.

50 Du Cerceau, op. cit. [note 22], pp. 212-13.

51 Ibid., pp. 272-3.

52 Ibid., pp. 274-5.

53 Ibid., p. 101.

54 Ibid., p. 173.

55 It could be argued that the castle style of Robert Adam, an architect who praised Vanbrugh, can be seen as an attempt to create a National Style following Vanbrugh's example.

5

Henry Keene and St Mary, Hartwell

Henry Keene and St Mary, Hartwell

Henry Keene and St Mary, Hartwell

Terry Friedman

IN 1750 Madame du Boccage visited Hartwell near Aylesbury in Buckinghamshire, the seat of Sir William Lee, the 4th Baronet (1726-99). She remarked that 'if a *Frenchman* had the same revenue of 70,000 livre a year, he would make much greater show than the master of this place'.[1] William's father, Thomas Lee, 3rd Baronet, commissioned James Gibbs between the early 1720s and 1740 to erect a series of garden buildings and remodel the hall of the Jacobean mansion, leaving the rest of the fabric unaltered.[2] Soon after inheriting the

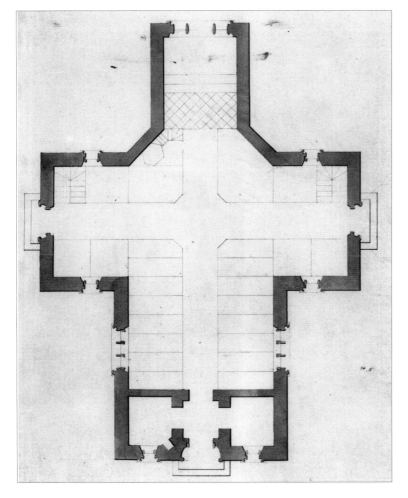

Opposite: west elevation, St Mary, Hartwell, 1753-5 (*English Heritage, National Monuments Record*, CC44/439, photographed 1943).

Left: Henry Keene, plan of the first design for St Mary, Hartwell, 1752 (*The Bodleian Library, University of Oxford*, MS. Top. Gen. B55, f. 29).

Henry Keene, west elevation of the first design for St Mary, Hartwell (*The Bodleian Library, University of Oxford*, MS. Top. Gen. B55, f. 31).

title on his father's death in 1749 William invited the fashionable London architect Henry Keene (1726-76) to overhaul the property, culminating in the remodelling between 1759 and 1763 of a substantial part of the mansion in a sophisticated late Palladian style.[3] Keene began, however, by replacing the nearby 15th-century parish church with a new structure which reveals an exceptional use of Gothic architecture. It was started in 1753 and completed within three years, but today it survives only as a pathetic shell, the result of having been abandoned in the 1940s and left to decay, as a distressing photographic survey by the National Monuments Record in 1942-3 reveals.[4] Yet, it still ignites our imagination.

The building accounts, now deposited in the Buckinghamshire Records and Local Studies Service, have inexplicably gone unnoticed until now (see appendices A-L).

They provide vividly detailed evidence of the designing and construction history of St Mary's, and also of the responsibilities of Keene's talented team of master craftsmen, which included his father, also Henry, a joiner, and the celebrated Oxford plasterer Thomas Roberts.[5] Six of these men are identified as 'London Tradesmen' (Appendix L) and inevitably there was a good deal of to-ing and fro-ing between there and Hartwell, some of the work being undertaken in the capital: for example, the ironmonger billed for 'fitting the Plates for the Pulpit door frame to the wood at Mr. Keenes Shop' (Appendix F). There was also co-operation between the work force, such as when the joiner charged for 'Making Molds for the [metal] Hinges and Latch' on the altar rail (Appendix B). The total cost of construction calculated on the principal bills was £2,443, with the architect charging a fee of £100 for making drawings and estimates, directing operations and for travel between 1753 and 1755 (Appendix A).

According to a faculty granted on December 20 1752, the medieval church was 'ruinous and decayed' and, as its patron, Lee proposed pulling it down and erecting 'a new one

Henry Keene, south elevation of the first design for St Mary, Hartwell (*The Bodleian Library, University of Oxford* MS. Top. Gen. B55, f. 32).

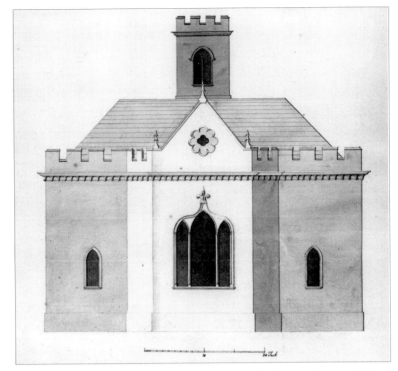

Henry Keene, east elevation of the first design for St Mary, Hartwell (*The Bodleian Library, University of Oxford* MS. Top. Gen. B55, f. 33).

Below:
Henry Keene, ceiling of the first design for St Mary, Hartwell (*The Bodleian Library, University of Oxford* MS. Top. Gen. B55, f. 34).

... at his own proper Costs ... some small distance' away.[6] The foundations and plumbing were laid in June 1753 (Appendix C).[7] The mason's bill is dated August 22 1754 and includes supplying 12,951 feet of 'Wadden Hill Stone' for 'plain Ashlour' and 'Molded work' and 4,436 feet of Totternhoe stone for window surrounds, cornices and string courses (Appendix I); both these are local whitish limestones which would have had the effect of setting off the building brilliantly in the landscape.[8] Further bills are dated December 5 1754, for wood carving (Appendix E); August 2 1755, for

supplying 743 feet 3 inches of Crown Glass (Appendix G);[9] and November 21 1755, for joinery totalling £305. 17s. 4d, probably representing the elder Keene's most substantial documented commission (Appendix B). Two receipts dated December 1755 and July 1756 relate to internal plaster-work,[10] which altogether totalled £576 (Appendix J). The masonry and joinery work were measured in August and September 1755 (Appendices D and B) and the majority of the bills were settled on November 21 of that year.

Set in a formal landscape dominated by Classical buildings, the richly Gothic gesture of this 'most beautiful small chapel'[11] might seem unexpected. However, William Lee's uncle, Sir George Lee, who contributed towards the cost of building the new church,[12] had been an undergraduate at Christ Church, Oxford, the college notable for the splendid Perpendicular fan-vaulted staircase (1638) of the College Hall and for Tom Tower's (*c*.1525) Gothic crown by Wren (1681-2).[13] By the time he was appointed Surveyor of the Fabric of Westminster in 1752, Keene had already established a reputation as a serious Gothicist. In 1749 he had redecorated the Bishop's chapel at Hartlebury Castle, Worcestershire, in a Gothic style, and this had attracted a commission in 1750 to supply the Dean and Chapter of Worcester with 'a draught of a proper Ornamental Portico in the Gothick Stile ... to be erected over the Great Gate' of the cathedral (unexecuted).[14]

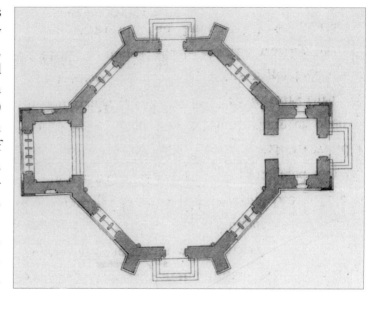

Plan of St Mary, Hartwell as built, 1753-5 (From W. H. Smyth, *Addenda to Aedes Hartwellianae* (1864)).

In 1752-3 Keene prepared two schemes for Hartwell, both itemised in Appendix A. The first, described only as 'a Design for a Church' and corresponding to the 'Plan' mentioned in the 1752 faculty,[15] can be identified with the set of six presentation drawings still among the Lee papers now in the Bodleian Library at Oxford.[16] It is for a box-like, battlemented, cruciform building with single- and triple-light windows and a timid tower riding the west end of the roof, just behind the gable. A small lobby, flanked by vestry rooms, leads into a short nave, shallow, galleried transepts with

South elevation, St Mary, Hartwell (*English Heritage, National Monuments Record*, A44/4408, photographed 1943).

canted walls forming an incipient octagon, and a deep, narrow, ill-lit chancel.

The difficulties of accommodating this awkward shape are revealed in the disconnected, rambling pattern of fan vaulting proposed for the ceiling.[17]

Some time early in 1753 Keene made a leap of architectural faith from this undemonstrative design to the inspired originality of the executed building.[18] He reformed the congregational space into a regular octagon, anchored between nearly identical projecting towers containing the chancel at the east end and an entrance lobby at the west end, with the Lee family pew above.[19] Two additional side entrances, a feature retained from the first design, now lead directly into the sides of the body, creating a dual-axiality with effectively three principal fronts of dramatically contrasting, hierarchial elevations. The western one, facing the churchyard, is the vertical frontispiece to the Lee family private entrance. The identical north and south elevations, facing the gardens and the mansion, used respectively by parishioners and by members of the household, are broader and flanked by pinnacle-capped, clasping buttresses and bracketed by twin towers. Hartwell stands out as the earliest octagonal church built in the Gothic Revival. Its generic model is almost certainly the medieval chapter house of Westminster Abbey,[20] and there is an uncanny resemblance

Plan & Elevation of the Gothic Cathedral.

J. H. Müntz, plan and elevation of the Gothic Cathedral at Kew, *c.*1759 (engraving in W. Chambers, *Plans, Elevations, Sections, and Perspective Views of the Gardens and Buildings at Kew in Surrey*, (London, 1763), pl. 29).

to J. H. Müntz's slightly later Gothic Cathedral at Kew.[21]

The radical new feature of the church as built was its ornamental intensity; in its heyday it was awash with exquisite detailing, as the bills make amply clear: 'Gothick Arches with Circular molded hollows', 'Gothick Groined Bracketing', 'Gothick Enricht Cornice' (Appendix B), '4 Gothick Cistron Heads [and] Gothic Pipe made in 3 shafts' (C), 'Gothick Roses' (E), '743 ft: 3 In. Sup Crown Glass ... cut in Gothic Figures' (G), '144 Crocketes on ye Pinikells' (H), 'Gothick Coping on Battlement And Buttress's' (K), and so on. The font, in the unusual form of clustered colonettes resembling compound piers, with a foliated cover, bears the

date 1756; though not itemised, it must surely be Keene Jr's creation. This customary attention to historic detail is confirmed in his 1769 specification for cloister gates at Westminster Abbey, which were to have 'figured Gothic pannells [and] framing nailed in Gothic figures wth: Gothic rose headed Nails'.[22] His method of harvesting authentic medieval motifs is revealed in a letter of 1766 dealing with alterations to the hall of University College, Oxford, describing how he had

Window, St Mary, Hartwell (*English Heritage, National Monuments Record*, A44/4414, photographed 1943).

several hands at work in London on the joiner's work: the Carving I will venture to affirm will please you, for tho' we talked about turning in order to be cheaper, I find it will not please me. I have therefore taken off casts in plaister at the Abbey, & shall have all the leaves all carv'd from these exactly, only of different sizes.[23]

Westminster Abbey would have been quarried in much the same way for the decoration at Hartwell.[24] The shallow, trilobe-ended panels on the towers' clasping buttresses are like those on the Abbey's west front. The quatrefoils clustered in threes and fives as window aprons, are found in many medieval tomb chests. [25] The pierced quatrefoil of the attic

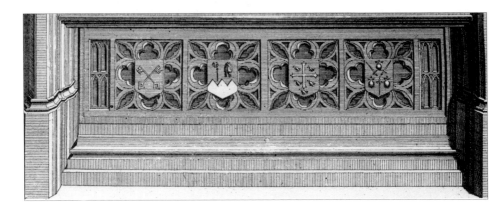

East elevation, St Mary, Hartwell (*English Heritage, National Monuments Record*, A44/4411, photographed 1943).

Opposite below: tomb of George Flaccet, Abbot of Westminster (J. Dart, *Westmonasterium, Or The History and Antiquities of the Abbey Church of St Peter's, Westminster*, I (London, 1723), p. 191).

windows and parapets is a Keene *leitmotif* which proliferates in the interior, including the extraordinary set of twelve 'Forms' or benches featuring 'Molded fronts to Seats', 'deal Ends with Molded fronts and Backs Cut to Shape' and '320 Holes Cut in ... for Ornaments' in the shape of polylobed rosettes (Appendix B). The introduction of lozenge-shaped transoms in the main windows, and 'sofits wrot: in many Gothick pannels' (Appendix J) in the internal west and east

arches, recalls John Dart's 1723 engraving of the Islip Chapel. The Perpendicular fan vaulting of Henry VII's Chapel (completed by 1509)[26] was the starting point for Thomas Robert's 'great Stucco Ceiling ... compleatly finished with Gothick Moldings and ornaments' (Appendix J), including a multitude of repeated radiating cusps, mouchettes and rosetted quatrefoils resembling some exquisite starry sky. Keene modified the medieval composition to fit his octagonal space by halving the eight outer fans, which spring from extravagantly slender, angle-engaged columns consisting of 'several shafts Enrich'd double Capitals ... and double Annulits' (Appendix J) and cluster around a huge, pendanted fan. A smaller version decorated the chancel vault.[27] Not since Wren's St Mary Aldermary in London (1679–82) had Perpendicular been exploited in a new church with such panache.[28]

Westminster Abbey was not Keene's only source of inspiration. The ogee and crocketed frames over the windows, inscription compartments, doors and arches of the west pew and chancel, all with 'Enrich'd Caps ... ornamented with moldings & foliage leaves' (Appendix J), can be traced to the octagonal

Opposite top: the Islip Chapel (J. Dart, *Westmonasterium, Or The History and Antiquities of the Abbey Church of St Peter's, Westminster*, I (London, 1723), p. 193 detail).

Opposite below: nave vault, St Mary, Hartwell, 1753-5 (*English Heritage, National Monuments Record*, A44/4416, photographed 1943).

Above: interior towards west door and Lee family pew, showing 1756 font, St Mary, Hartwell (*English Heritage, National Monuments Record*, CC44/437, photographed 1943).

Above: interior towards north, St Mary, Hartwell (*English Heritage, National Monuments Record*, CC44/434, photographed 1943).

Opposite: chancel vault, St Mary, Hartwell (*English Heritage, National Monuments Record*, A44/4417, photographed 1942).

Henry Keene and St Mary, Hartwell

Market Cross (1501) at Chichester in Sussex, which had undergone repairs in 1746 by the architect William Ride, who also drew the building for an engraving issued by the Society of Antiquaries of London in 1749.[29] This large, splendid image, in which the west and south fronts of the Cross are displayed as diptych-like vignettes, may have prompted the expansive layout of the Hartwell altarpiece. Here the communion table and its wings are flanked by twin inscription panels attached to the side walls of the chancel, a *tour de force* of Georgian Gothic church furnishing described in considerable detail in the joiner's, carver's and ironmonger's bills (Appendices B, E, F).[30]

We now come to the real surprise presented in these bills. Despite the profusion of 'Rich Gothick' motifs on the altarpiece, specified by the carver (Appendix E), the elder Keene's bill describes an 'Altar all of Rt. Wainscot in the Saxon manner the Moldings Composed of small unusual Members', with a further entry referring to 'very Small Members in thickness' (Appendix B), implying squat, Romanesque-like columns. Moreover, Keene Jr billed for 'Making a Second Design in the Saxon Manner' for the church, which included 'several Extraordinary drawings [untraced], Directions, & Journeys ... occasion'd by Alterations, & Additions, to the Church &ca. more than was intended, at the making the above Agreement' (Appendix A). This 'Second Design' is for the church as built.

As an architectural term, the Georgians used 'Saxon' imprecisely to describe features of the pre-Conquest, Norman and early Gothic periods. For Wren, the 'round Pillars round headed Arches, and Windows' of 10th-century

Interior towards chancel, St Mary, Hartwell (*English Heritage, National Monuments Record*, CC44/436, photographed 1943).

Opposite top: George Vertue after William Ride, 'The Market Cross at Chichester' (engraving, 1749: *author's collection*).

Opposite below: tomb of Sebert, King of the East Saxons (J. Dart, *Westmonsterium, Or The History and Antiquities of the Abbey Church of St Peter's, Westminster*, I (London, 1723), p. 4 detail).

Westminster Abbey epitomised the 'ancient Saxon Manner'.[31] The antiquary William Stukeley described 12th-century Norman Durham Cathedral as a 'majestic pile, of the Saxon manner of building intirely', explaining that 'I call that the Saxon manner which was in use among us at the time of the Conquest; being somewhat Roman degenerate, with semicircular windows, and arches and great round pillars, the walls very thick, without buttresses'.[32] Thomas Warton described 13th-century (Early English) Salisbury Cathedral as being in the 'Saxon Stile' or 'a sort of Gothic Saxon'.[33]

One might suggest that the singularly 'Saxon' feature at Hartwell is the polylobed, radial-traceried, blind wheel-windows, itemised in the stonecutter's bill as '4 Large Roses'

(Appendix H), which appear in the first design as a hesitant miniature motif; in the second they are prominently placed in expanses of flat, undecorated wall on all four elevations. The shape is close to 11th- and 12th-century examples found throughout Europe, and while there is no conclusive evidence of what Keene had in mind, the distinguished example of St Nicholas, Barfreston in Kent had been recorded in 1749 in a manuscript folio entitled 'Drawings of Saxon Churches' compiled by Charles Lyttelton, the Dean of Exeter.[34] In the same year, Keene was assisting Sanderson Miller in preparing designs for Hagley Hall in Worcestershire, the seat of George, 1st Baron Lyttelton, the Dean's older

brother.[35] A note in the manuscript in the Dean's hand states that 'This is ye only Collection of Saxon Buildings that Ever was made' and refers to the examples as:

Henry Keene, plan and elevation for a Gothic Temple at Hartwell, undated (*The Bodleian Library, University of Oxford*, MS. Top. Gen. B55, f. 14).

Executed in the Style of Architecture which prevail'd here in the Saxon & first Norman Ages, before the introduction of the Gothick, and which, however confounded with the Gothick by ye generality of our Writers on Antiquitys, yet in fact, is no other than a debased & corupt Roman Architecture.

It should be noted that the Hartwell wheel windows have an additional central rosette, which also appears in the quatrefoils of the window aprons, pews and chancel railing. This distinctive motif occurs in the Westminster Abbey tomb of Sebert, King of the East Saxons, which in the 10th-century building had been a plain burial chest but, following its resiting after 1307 in the new south ambulatory, it was placed in a niche embellished with rosetted quatrefoils. When Dart illustrated the tomb in 1723 he cited early histories crediting Sebert (died 616) with founding the Abbey in 605 after having demolished the Roman temple of Apollo on the same site.[36] At Hartwell, the unexpected appearance of the new church amidst the Classical elysium of Gibbs's garden may well have carried a similiar symbolic message of Christian triumphalism over the pagans.

There is even more poignant evidence of Keene's intentions. Among the Lee papers in the Bodleian Library is an undated and unexecuted proposal in his hand for an elaborately detailed Gothic garden pavilion, which is itself a reworking of his record drawing of the Gothic Temple at Shotover in Oxfordshire, designed and built earlier in the 18th century by the Oxford architect William Townesend, for

Henry Keene, plan and elevation of the Gothic Temple at Shotover, Oxfordshire, undated (*The Bodleian Library, University of Oxford*, MS. Top. Gen. B55, f. 13).

East front of St Nicholas, Barfreston, Kent, 1749, from Charles Lyttelton's MS. 'Drawings of Saxon Churches' (*Society of Antiquaries of London*).

the medieval historian James Tyrell.[37] Here, a 'Saxon' wheel window is combined with Early English arches, niches, battlements and pinnacles in a composition which clarifies Keene's use of the phrase 'in the Saxon Manner' as a Wartonian 'sort of Gothic Saxon'.

Though they have often admired it as 'a beautiful Gothic church',[38] modern historians have persistently miscategorised Hartwell as a creation of those 'carefree days' of rococo Gothic,[39] or as 'a classical design in fancy dress'[40] by an architect who 'had no real understanding of Gothic'.[41] On the contrary, Keene can now be seen as an unconventional and courageous pioneer in promoting the style for new churches and Hartwell as at the very heart of the mid-18th century attempts to create a progressive ecclesiastical Gothic based on historical authenticity entirely free of Classical associations, and furthermore as an avant–garde masterpiece.

Acknowledgements
I am grateful to the Bodleian Library, University of Oxford; Buckinghamshire Records and Local Studies Service; English Heritage (National Monuments Record); Society of Antiquaries, London; Warwickshire Record Office; and Westminster Abbey Library, for permission to publish material in their keeping; and to Dr Derek Linstrum and Eric R. Throssell for help in preparing this article.

Notes
1 M. F. Boccage, *Letters Concerning England, Holland and Italy*, (London, 1770), volume 1, p. 66.
2 Terry Friedman, *James Gibbs* (New Haven and London, 1984), pp. 182, 184-9, 200, 291-2, plates 204-11, 220.

3 Christopher Hussey, *English Country Houses: Early Georgian 1715-1760* (London, 1955), pp. 200-3; Gervase Jackson-Stops, 'Hartwell House, Buckinghamshire', *Country Life*, November 22, 1990, pp. 68-73. The fullest account of Hartwell and the Lees is W. H. Smyth, *Aedes Hartwellianae, or Notices of the Manor and Mansion of Hartwell* (London, 1851).

4 The report in 'Notes', *Records of Buckinghamshire*, 15, part 2 (1948), p. 144, makes miserable reading: 'Hartwell is the most remarkable church of its kind in the country [though now] derelict and unused ... The first damage was caused ... by sheer laziness and neglect of the ... churchwarden to keep the church gutters and rain pipes clear of obstacles and in good repair ... the water has run down and through the walls ... most of the plaster vault over the sanctuary has fallen, together with a large area of that over the nave; the service books ... remain mildewed and tattered', though a proposal to demolish was 'fortunately stopped'.

5 The slater, using 'Best westmerland Slateing', was John Westcott of Gray's Inn Lane, London (Buckinghamshire Records Office and Local Studies Service, henceforth BRO, PR 96/7/1). Geoffrey Beard, *Craftsmen and Interior Decoration in England 1660-1820* (Edinburgh, 1981), pp. 250, 252, 257, 278-9, 286, 290, and *Decorative Plasterwork in Great Britain* (London, 1975), pp. 235-6, plate 82; Howard Colvin, *A Biographical Dictionary of British Architects 1600-1840* (New Haven and London, 1995), pp. 571-4; H. Clifford Smith, 'Henry Keene: A Georgian Architect', *Country Life*, March 30, 1945, p. 556, figure 1, a lost conversation picture by Robert Pyle, 1760, depicting Keene Jr, William Cobbett and Thomas Dryhurst, among others.

6 BRO, D/LE/D13/19. The old church is glimpsed in Nebot's 1738 view (Friedman, op. cit. [note 2], pls. 204, 208, 210). Demolition is recorded in D/LE/D13/15, ff. 1,7).

7 Also BRO, D/LE/D13/10, account of Abraham King, smith, 1753-5.

8 Nikolaus Pevsner and Elizabeth Williamson, *The Buildings of England: Buckinghamshire* (London, 1994), pp. 24, 27, plate 73.

9 On August 27 1755 17*s*. was charged for 'pointing 34 window frams' (BRO, D/LE/D13/15, f. 6).

10 'Decemr. ye 2d 1755 Recd: of Sr: William Lee Bart. Three hundred pounds on acct: of Stucco work at Hartwell p me Thos Roberts' (BRO, D/LE/D13/13); 'July ye 13th 1756 Recd: of Sr: William Lee, Bart:, by the hands of Spencer Schutz Esqr: Two Hundred & Twenty Nine Pounds in full of all demands for Stuccowork in Hartwell Church, p me Thomas Roberts' (BRO, D/LE/D13/14).

11 J. J. Cartwright (editor), *The Travels Through England of Dr. Richard Pococke Successively Bishop of Meath and Ossory during 1750, 1751, and Later Years*, The Camden Society, New Series, 2, volume 44 (1889), p. 241, a visit dated October 5 1756.

12 Sir George Lee and another uncle gave £1,500. Smyth, op. cit. [note 3], pp. 11-12, 96.

13 Geoffrey Tyack, *Oxford: An Architectural Guide* (Oxford and New York, 1998), pp. 113, 141-2.

14 Worcester Cathedral Muniments, A78, Chapter Act Book 1747-79, f. 19, 18 May 1750. Michael McCarthy, *The Origins of the Gothic Revival* (New Haven and London, 1987), p. 154, plates 197-8; Timothy Mowl, 'Henry Keene, 1726-1776: A Goth in Spite of Himself' in R. Brown (editor), *The Architectural Outsiders* (London, 1985), pp. 87, 213-14.

15 'Plan of the Building hereunto Annexed' (BRO, D/LE/D13/19), now elsewhere (see note 16).

16 MS. Top. Gen. B55, ff. 29, 30 (vault plan), 31, 32, 33, 34. McCarthy, op. cit. [note 14], p.196 note 28, wrongly claims that these designs 'seem to be later in date, drawings after the building rather than for it'.

17 The design resembles Shobdon (1746-56), currently attributed to the patron, Richard Bateman, collaborating with William Kent. Joan Lane, 'Shobdon Church, Herefordshire: A Rococo Gothic masterpiece', *Apollo*, January 1995, pp. 23-7; McCarthy, op. cit. [note 14], pp. 151-4, plates 192-3.

18 McCarthy's claim that the elaborately detailed design in the Victoria and Albert Museum (op. cit. [note 14], p. 157, plates 200-1) represents a preliminary scheme for Hartwell, from which he concludes that the church as built 'represents a process of simplification of ornament ... which may partly be accounted for by the difficulty of finding competent carvers and masons in the gothic style' is contradicted by the evidence of both the bills and the building itself. The small size and lack of liturgical provisions makes plates 200-1 an unlikely candidate for a church; nor can plates 202-3 (p. 158) be specifically associated with Hartwell.

19 The church measures 16 feet on each side by 64 feet high, and the towers are 88 feet high (Smyth, op. cit. [note 3], p.12).

20 Smyth, op. cit. [note 3], p.12, cites on no authority York Minster chapter house as the source. Keene may have noticed 'The Ichonography of the Cathedral Church of Ely' in Browne Willis, *A Survey of the Cathedrals of Lincoln, Ely, Oxford and Peterborough* (London, 1730), following p. 330, recording the liturgical arrangement of the crossing prior to James Essex's 1759-72 remodelling (Philip Lindley, '"Carpenter Gothic" and Gothic Carpentry:

Contrasting Attitudes to the Restoration of the Octagon and Removals of the Choir at Ely Cathedral', *Architectural History*, 30 (1987), pp. 98-104, figures 11-12, in which the eight piers, connected by dotted lines, together with the western lobby-like space screened from the Romanesque nave and the altar space extended into but walled-off from the presbytery, form a perimeter configuration remarkably similiar to Hartwell's. Smyth, op. cit. [note 3], p. 11, notes Willis's manuscript description of old Hartwell church in the Bodleian Library, Oxford.

21 Dated *c*.1759. (John Harris, 'Chambers's Design for the Gothic Cathedral at Kew', *The Georgian Group Journal*, 8 (1998), pp. 151-6, figure 2).

22 Westminster Abbey Library, WAM 24836, f.16v.

23 Warwickshire County Record Office, CR 136B/1785. McCarthy, op. cit. [note 14], fig.174.

24 Thomas Cocke, *900 Years: the Restoration of Westminster Abbey* (London, 1995), which includes a discussion of Keene's contributions.

25 Similiar aprons were used by Sanderson Miller at Radway Grange, Warwickshire (1746): McCarthy, op. cit. [note 14], pl.152.

26 W. C. Leedy Jr, *Fan Vaulting, a Study of Form, Technology, and Meaning* (London, 1980), pp. 214-17, plates 49, 82, 212-14.

27 Keene previously experimented with fan vaulting at Hartlebury Castle chapel; the Museum at Enville Hall, Staffordshire (*c*.1750); and perhaps the Great Hall, Welbeck Abbey, Nottinghamshire (1751): Mowl, op. cit. [note 14], p. 84, plates 68, 70; Giles Worsley, *Classical Architecture in Britain: the Heroic Age* (New Haven and London, 1995), p. 193, figure 222.

28 Simon Bradley and Nikolaus Pevsner, *The Buildings of England London: The City Churches* (London, 1998), pp. 106-7, plate 36.

29 Ride (*c*.1723-78) resided during part of his career in Westminster (Colvin, op. cit. [note 5], p. 817).

30 On 10 August 1816, N. Hoskins estimated 'to alter Tabletts in Chancel by taking down present Pediments - making good ground work putting up Gothic ribs to form Arch with enriched Crotchetts ornament Crowns &c. to match present wood' (BRO, PR 96/7/1); he was also to 'Colour [the] Kings Arms' in the Lee pew, which are not itemized in the bills and may be post-1755 embellishment. There is no record of these and other 'Repairs' having been done following the residency of the exiled French court, 1810-14: *The Victoria History of the County of Buckinghamshire*, (London, 1908), volume 2, p. 294.

31 Quoted in Stephen Wren, *Parentalia: or, Memoirs of the Family of Wren* (London, 1750), p. 296. The building was stylistically

Romanesque.

32 W. Stukeley, *Itinerarum Curiosum: or, an Account of the Antiquities, and Remarkable Curiosities in Nature or Art Observed in Travels Through Great Britain* (London, 1776), volume 2, p. 70, entry dated 1725.

33 T. Warton, *Observations on The Faerie Queen of Spenser*, 2 (second edition, London, 1762), p. 186. This building was celebrated in Francis Price, *A Series of Particular and Useful Observations, Made with Great Diligence and Care, upon that Admirable Structure, The Cathedral-Church of Salisbury* (London, 1753), the first serious architectural study of a Gothic building.

34 The folio, presented by the Dean to the Society of Antiquaries of London in 1782, contains drawings dated between 1733 and 1753, with a note in his hand, 'This Book contains several original Drawings, for the most part taken from the Door Ways &c of English Country Churches' (Thomas Cocke and C.R. Dodwell, 'Rediscovery of the Romanesque' in *1066: English Romanesque Art 1066-1200* (London, 1984), pp. 47, 362, 373 no.512). In 1742 the Dean read a paper to the Society on the differences between the Saxon and Norman styles (McCarthy, op. cit. [note 14], p. 23). Colin Platt, *The Architecture of Medieval Britain: a Social History* (New Haven and London, 1990), plate 42.

35 Mowl, op. cit. [note 14], p. 214.

36 J. Dart, *Westmonasterium* (London, 1723), volume 1, pp. 3-7. Francis Bond, *Westminster Abbey* (Oxford, 1909), p. 3, illustration.

37 Tyrell's father had come from Oakley, nine miles west of Hartwell: Jennifer Sherwood and Nikolaus Pevsner, *The Buildings of England: Oxfordshire* (Harmondsworth, 1974), pp. 763-5. McCarthy, op. cit. [note 14], p. 27, plate 22; Mavis Batey, 'Shotover's Continuity with the Past', *Country Life*, December 29 1977, pp. 1978-9.

38 Kenneth Clark, *The Gothic Revival* (London, 1928; 1964 edition), p. 78.

39 Terence Davis, *The Gothick Taste* (Newton Abbot, 1974), pp. 91, 138, plates 66-7.

40 Marcus Whiffen, *Stuart and Georgian Churches* (London, 1948), p. 70, plate 86.

41 G. McHardy, in S. C. Humphrey (editor), *Blue Guide: Churches and Chapels of Southern England* (London, 1991), p. 113. John Betjeman and John Piper, *Murray's Buckinghamshire Architectural Guide* (London, 1948), p. 119, plates 121-3, describe it as 'neither Gothic nor Classical, but Romantic'.

6

'The ivi'd ruins of folorn Grace Dieu': Catholics, Romantics and late Georgian Gothic

Catholics, Romantics and late Georgian Gothic

'The ivi'd ruins of folorn Grace Dieu': Catholics, Romantics and late Georgian Gothic[1]

Rosemary Hill

IN HIS FAMOUS sermon on the Catholic Revival, 'The Second Spring', John Henry Newman recalled how, in his Evangelical youth, he had imagined the old religion: 'An old-fashioned house of gloomy appearance, closed in with high walls, with an iron gate and yews, and the report ... that Roman Catholics lived there.' [2]

A remarkably similar picture came into the mind of a fellow Tractarian and convert, Frederick Oakley, when he too looked back at his early impressions of the English Catholics: 'a large haunted house embosomed in yew trees ... walled with tapestry ... enormous beds with ebony bedsteads surmounted by plumes and a preternatural silence broken only by the flapping of bats and the screeching of owls.'[3] No wonder Gladstone thought that Walter Scott should be given a place in the history of the Catholic Revival.[4] To most English people in the early 19th century, Roman Catholicism was by definition medieval: it had not been openly practised in England since the 16th century. Until Catholic Emancipation in 1829, and for some time afterwards, the English tended to form their ideas about it from Gothic novels and poetry. This was true to some extent of Catholics themselves and it was certainly the case with many converts.

The popular prejudice against 'Popery' was partially broken down by the image of the Middle Ages in the works of Scott. The impression of 'vividly described characters moving against a background of Gothic architecture' went deep into the national imagination.[5] Scott added light and colour to the paraphernalia of glamorous gloom, the yews and bats of 18th-century Gothic. He animated the past with a cheerier, more robust picture of England in 'the olden times'.

Opposite: Augustus Welby Northmore Pugin *c.*1833 by an unknown artist *(National Portrait Gallery).*

St Peter's Chapel,
Winchester,
Hampshire J. Cave and
J. Pass, 1809.

Thus the Catholic Revival, like the Gothic Revival, enjoyed its Waverley phase. By the time of the Second Spring sermon in July 1852 it was over. What brief sympathy Newman himself had felt for Gothic architecture was long passed. The idea that Gothic was a uniquely Catholic style was as fanciful to him as *Ivanhoe* and less interesting. His sermon, however, was preached at Oscott College, a building that bore witness to the intensity with which the ideal of Catholic Gothic had once been pursued and where A. W. N. Pugin had first attempted to put into practice the vision he expressed in *Contrasts*.

Catholics, Romantics and late Georgian Gothic

That this was a vision that had more to do with English history and the Romantic movement than with the Roman Catholic church itself is one argument I would like to make here. It is sometimes said to be ironic that it was the High Church and the Anglo-Catholics who took Pugin's message most to heart. In fact it was quite natural, for it was from an Anglican tradition that it came in the first place, the tradition in which Pugin himself grew up. He absorbed from childhood the English view of Catholicism as medieval, suspended in time, 'dimly seen as in a mist or through twilight', as Newman put it. [6]

Pugin's belief that Gothic was the only true Catholic style had its roots in the writings of the English antiquaries and its flowering in Romanticism, when reaction to the Enlightenment and the French Revolution made such intense identification with the Middle Ages prevalent across the whole of northern Europe. He is usually seen as the nemesis of Georgian architecture, the herald of the Victorian Gothic Revival. This of course he was. Yet his vision was as much the culmination of a Georgian theme as the first statement of a Victorian one.

This chapter looks back over the period when the idea of Gothic architecture as Catholic emerged, or rather re-emerged, in English antiquarianism and became imbued with Romanticism and the Picturesque. These are the years from about 1792 to 1836, from the building of Milner's St Peter's chapel in Winchester to the publication of Pugin's *Contrasts*. In following the train of ideas that had the greatest influence on Pugin and hence on English architecture we find ourselves involved in an episode of local, even provincial history. The great figures of European Romanticism - Goethe, Schlegel, Chateaubriand - here play minor roles, their ideas coming to the English Gothic Revival late and filtered through other imaginations.

This was so partly because English antiquarianism had its own peculiar intellectual tradition, distinguished but isolated. Antiquarian studies began in this country with the Reformation. Antiquaries were by no means all Catholics, though some were, and many were High Church. None were Puritan, for the simple reason, as Graham Parry says, that

Title page of
Monasticon Anglicanum
by Wenceslaus Hollar
to a design by William
Dugdale, 1655.

what the Puritans destroyed was the antiquaries' stock in trade.[7] The fact that Gothic architecture was the creation of a pre-Reformation Catholic society was a self-evident truth. The suspicion that the study of it implied a sympathy with the old religion was an idea that came and went. It tended to come in periods of social and religious disturbance when the writing of any kind of history became politically charged.

With the Dissolution of the monasteries still just within living memory Walter Raleigh recalled the time when so 'great an increase ... of Sectaries in this Realm' had meant that all cost and care bestowed and had of the church wherein God is to be served ... was accounted ... a kinde of Popery; so that the time would soon bring it to passe ... that God would be turned out of churches into Barnes ... and church government left to newness of opinion and men's fancies ... as many kinds of Religion springing up, as there are parish-churches ... in England.'[8]

Such was again the situation in the lifetime of the greatest of the Stuart antiquaries, William Dugdale. A High-Church Royalist, writing during and after the Civil War, Dugdale read the crisis of his own time by the light of the Dissolution. He used it as a metaphor or antetype, taking Raleigh's words for the epigraph to his *History of St Paul's* published in 1656. Dugdale's greatest work, the *Monasticon Anglicanum* (1655-73), is a monumental elegy, a lament for the religious and social institutions of the Middle Ages and at the same time a plea for the surviving churches and cathedrals threatened with destruction by Puritanism.

Dugdale's concern was with social and political rather than purely architectural history, yet the *Monasticon* included 'the most accurate engravings of Church architecture that had ever appeared in an English book'.[9] They were by Wenceslaus Hollar. Hollar also drew a title page to Dugdale's design that proclaimed through its iconography his political and religious position. At the top, Henry III re-endorses Magna Carta, below him stand the figures of Gregory and Augustine, founders of Christianity in England, while on the plinths are a pair of vignettes that must be particularly striking to anyone who knows Pugin's *Contrasts*.[10] On the left, a pious king, offering his donation to an abbey, appears against a background of peace and social order. On the right Henry VIII proclaims '*sic volo*' and the abbey and the society it represented lie in ruins.

Dugdale was not of course a Roman Catholic. His title page makes the case for the English Catholic church, a church whose independence of state control was given in Magna Carta and brutally and illegally taken by Henry VIII. The source of its authority is not the Crown but its continuity with the pre-Reformation traditions of the early

Church. This is represented by Augustine and Gregory and, beyond them, by Glastonbury Abbey (in the top left hand corner of the title page) and its supposed founder, Joseph of Arimathaea.

This High-Church perspective informed a great deal of English antiquarian scholarship. Those, like Pugin, who grew up with the works of Dugdale simply absorbed it as history. It is the premise of the first edition of *Contrasts* that Gothic architecture flourished up until the Reformation, when the change of religion destroyed it at a stroke. Pugin did not mention the Renaissance because he knew nothing about it. It played no part in English antiquarian histories, in which the Reformation was always the defining event.

In the 1820s and 1830s the tradition that Dugdale represented, never entirely dormant, became important again. The authority and identity of the English Church came into question once more and Raleigh's words were uncannily apt. 'Newness of opinion' was rife and 'men's fancies' ran wild indeed. These years saw the worst civil unrest in English history. Religious division brought fears of social disintegration. The spectre of revolution was not far from anyone's mind. Sects abounded, private judgment set itself up against religious authority, Catholic Emancipation challenged the position of the established church and millenarianism was so widespread that 'prophecy became a normal intellectual activity in ... England'.[11]

A new, extended edition of the *Monasticon Anglicanum* was published in eight volumes between 1817 and 1830. This was no doubt largely a response to the growing interest in antiquarianism, but it had all the same a High-Church bias. It was edited between London and Oxford. Among the subscribers were several of Pugin's future patrons but not one fellow or college library from Cambridge, a fact which suggests that the political and religious implications of the *Monasticon* were still perfectly well understood in the early 19th century.

So it was that the hint or taint of Catholic sympathy was never far from English antiquarianism. In 1797 when James Wyatt failed to be elected to the Society of Antiquaries George III denounced the members as a 'Popish Cabal'.[12]

Catholics, Romantics and late Georgian Gothic

The King made it clear that the Society should vote again and keep voting until they got an acceptable result. He was of course virulent, even paranoid, in his fear of Catholicism but in this case he was also right. The Society's principal objection to Wyatt was architectural and unanswerable, that he had spoiled Salisbury Cathedral. But an important, highly articulate objector was John Milner, a Catholic priest.

After the first ballot, Milner had written a *Dissertation on the Modern Style of Altering Antient Cathedrals*, a critical account of Wyatt's work at Salisbury, which he submitted to the Society. The Antiquaries effectively suppressed it, holding on to the text until after the second (successful) vote. A year later, when Milner's *History of Winchester* had been published and disowned by the Society, he lost patience and published the *Dissertation* himself. This prompted a burst of attacks, counter-attacks and learned appendices which went on for years and were still being reprinted in the 1840s, long after Milner's death.

Milner saw himself explicitly in the tradition of Dugdale. Like Dugdale, he considered himself to be writing at 'a critical period for the science of antiquity' and, like the Stuart antiquaries, he wrote about buildings in the context of the society that had produced them, offering motives, causes and consequences', not just a 'bare rehearsal of insulated facts.'[13] For this, he was accused of 'enveloping a question of mere taste in the dark clouds of religious controversy.'[14] Milner was a gifted scholar, open but unpolemical in his Catholicism. His reasonableness only made him more exasperating to the Anglican clergy, whose buildings and history he understood so much better than they. 'If [the clergy] will not be good Catholics', Milner coolly explained, 'I am desirous that they should remain good Church of England men ... I wish to prevent them from frittering away their religion.'[15]

The *History of Winchester* made the same metaphorical connection between social and architectural fabric as Dugdale. It did so most controversially in an attack on the late Bishop Hoadly, that 'champion of liberty and the low church' whose monument was – and still is – cut deep into a shaft at the east end of the nave of Winchester Cathedral.[16]

'Moat House, Ightham, Kent, the Chapel' by Joseph Nash, from *The Mansions of England in the Olden Time* (London, 1839-40).

'Thus it may be said of Hoadly', Milner wrote, that 'both living and dying he undermined the church of which he was a prelate.'[17] This was the sort of satire that thrilled Pugin when he read it 30 years later and, like Dugdale, Milner was an important influence on *Contrasts*. Pugin admired him almost to the point of devotion.

Had he lived, however, Milner would not have returned the compliment. He was a man of his time, a late Augustan not a Romantic, his aesthetic authority is Burke on the Sublime, the poets he invokes are Milton and Grey. Nevertheless, in Milner we find the first stirrings of that romantic idea, so potent to the next generation, that Gothic buildings are expressive, that they embody their own meaning. It is with him that the idea of Catholic Gothic architecture begins to turn from an historical fact to a present, living reality. Milner had no doubt that the correct character of a Gothic cathedral was not to be beauty but psychological and emotional power, the capacity to create 'religious awe'.[18] The 'aspiring form of the pointed arches' produced he thought an 'artificial infinite' in the mind of the spectator.[19] In particular he argued for the importance and ecclesiological correctness of screens, for the effect of discrete internal spaces, 'sequestered, awful - fit for contemplation.'[20]

Milner's *History of Winchester* concludes with a description of his own church, St Peter's, of 1792. This was designed by his friend and fellow antiquary John Carter in the Gothic style that was 'the perfection of ecclesiastical architecture.'[21] It was intended as a deliberate criticism of the modern style of church building, 'the small sashed windows and fashionable decorations, hardly to be distinguished ... from common assembly rooms'.[22] It is not, in architectural terms, prodigiously advanced for its date. With its plaster vaults and wooden pinnacles there is nothing to add here to what others have said of it as a building. [23] Its significance lies not in its structure but in its intention, which was to reanimate, physically, the tradition of English Catholic architecture, to mend the broken continuity of history.

Milner's *History* is in two volumes. The detailed, loving account of his chapel is attached not to the first, a chronological history continued up to the present time, but to the second, 'the Survey of the Antiquities'. Milner did not include his chapel with the new buildings, the shops, the theatre, or the silk manufacture, but as a duly modest coda to the descriptions of the cathedral, the Hospital of St Cross and the other medieval buildings of Winchester. This was how he saw his chapel. It was not important as modern architecture. Its value lay in its associative powers, its relationship to the Middle Ages, and its ability to evoke 'pleasing and awful sensations'.[24] This was an idea that belonged to early romanticism more than antiquarianism. It would have baffled Dugdale.

At his death, in 1826, when he was a bishop and Vicar Apostolic of the Midland District, Milner bequeathed £1,000 for a Gothic church to be built by Joseph Ireland in Wolverhampton. In the event, St Peter and St Paul was built in the Classical style, Pugin's brass striking the only discordant Gothic note in its interior. It is not clear why the design was changed, but the reason is less important than the fact, which serves to indicate that the Gothic tradition had no deep roots in the main body of the Roman Catholic church.

The year that Milner died saw the full force of

continental Romantic Catholicism unleashed on the English reading public when Kenelm Digby published the second edition of his curious work *The Broadstone of Honour*. In the interval since the first edition, Digby, an Irish Protestant by birth, had become a Catholic. The influence of Scott and Southey, Chateaubriand, Schlegel and his own peculiar imagination had made of Digby something between Lord Byron and Lewis Carroll's White Knight. He had fought a lion, he had dived into the Rhine, yet he was a gentle, slender man whose extravagance and prolixity in print contrasted with a retired and uneventful private life.

Digby was never as widely read as Scott's work and has been more quickly and more thoroughly forgotten. In its day, however, *The Broadstone of Honour* was admired by many, from the aging Wordsworth to the young Burne-Jones.[25] It portrayed medieval Christendom as a golden age, the Reformation as a death blow to its social as well as its religious values. Yet it was not a history so much as a manual, a handbook to chivalry, which Digby wanted and expected to see revive as Milner hoped that architecture would.

Where architecture was concerned, Digby epitomised the conflation of antiquarianism with late-Georgian aesthetics. His theories were cruder than Milner's but he went further. 'A distinguishing characteristic of everything belonging to the early and middle ages of Christianity is the picturesque' he explained.[26] 'As soon as men renounced the philosophy of the Church it was inevitable that their taste ... should change ... For architects had no longer to provide for the love of solitude, of meditation between sombre pillars, of modesty in apartments with the lancet casement ... the ... sombre arches were to ... make way for ... a blaze of light which might correspond with the mind of those who rejected every proposition that led beyond the reach of the senses and who wished to believe that there was nothing in the world but what they saw and touched.'[27]

In other words, the Enlightenment had light buildings. Dark buildings were for people who believed in more than they could see. It was simple, far too simple, but, spun out in the airy prose of *The Broadstone of Honour*, Digby's thin philosophy glittered like beaten gold in the eyes of his

romantic readership. I imagine, though I cannot be sure, that Pugin read *The Broadstone of Honour* and perhaps he looked at the much longer and less popular *Mores Catholici* which followed, volume after volume over two decades. Certainly, Pugin met Digby soon after his own conversion to Catholicism. Pugin's son Edward Welby designed a chantry chapel for the Digby family at his father's church, St Augustine's, Ramsgate. Digby, however, chose not to be buried there, a fact to which we will return.

Among the protagonists of the early Catholic Revival

on whom Digby had a decisive personal influence was Ambrose Phillipps. Phillipps was a generation younger than Digby. He had become a Catholic at the age of 16, to the horror of his family, especially his Whig father. On a visit to Paris, Phillipps was inspired by the sight of Mass being celebrated. At home again in Leicestershire he was reproached by God in a dream for not following his conscience. Forthwith he arranged to be received at the cottage of an Irish paviour, into a Church of which he knew nothing but that it was true.

As an undergraduate at Cambridge Phillipps met Digby, who had been allowed to keep rooms at Trinity, his Catholicism being regarded by that university as mere harmless eccentricity (non-Conformists could matriculate at Cambridge, unlike Oxford, even though they could not take a degree). Phillipps was an emotional, at times hysterical young man, whose religious vision was cast in the prophetic, millenarian terms so pervasive in those days. He entered deeply into Digby's chivalric ideal, an ideal which was social as much as religious. Phillipps's High Toryism was as antipathetic to his father as his Catholicism. The Catholic society Phillipps envisaged was, like Digby's, a benign, paternalistic hierarchy.

The same dream, a morally-charged version of the Olden Times, had come to Pugin before he knew Phillipps, and before he became either a Catholic or a practising architect. He drew several 'ideal schemes', sequences of scenes, part architectural, part narrative. In a drawing of about 1832 he illustrated the relationship of architecture to church and state in this perfect once-and-future world. The architect explains his designs respectfully to an array of appreciative clergy and laity. Such moments were to be rare in Pugin's career. Both he and Phillipps often found difficulty in making the real Roman Catholic clergy play the roles they had so clearly envisaged for them.

The Romantic Catholic ideal embraced every aspect of private and family life as well as work and worship. It had a powerful erotic charge, which was chivalric and heterosexual, in contrast to the homoeroticism of the later Anglo-Catholic Gothic Revival. 'The husband ... in the castle with his wife and children around him': this was the pattern offered by Digby's *Mores Catholici* and both Phillipps and Pugin aspired to that ideal.[28] They saw their wives as companions and helpers. The value given to women in medieval society was one reason Digby gave for its superiority to Classical civilization.

With Phillipps, the idea of Catholic Gothic became fully romantic in the sense that it allowed for no distinction between subjective and objective experience. Like Pugin, he wanted to inhabit the world of his religious vision in the most literal way. The Catholic Revival meant, to him, the physical rebuilding of Catholic England. In 1835 he attended the consecration of Scoles's chapel at Stonyhurst. As plainchant once again echoed through the aisles of a Catholic Gothic church, he felt that he was present at 'an epoch in the Catholick history of England'.[29]

After his marriage to Laura Clifford in 1833 he began to build his own 'ideal scheme', a Catholic christendom in 19th-century Leicestershire; house, school, monastery and church near his family home in what was then remote and wild countryside. The estate included the land belonging to Grace Dieu, the medieval convent on whose 'ivie'd ruins' Wordsworth meditated in 1811: 'Communities are lost, and Empires die,/And things of holy use unhallowed lie.'[30] Sweet regret and melancholy: that was one romantic mood appropriate to the medieval ruin. The other was a vision of rebirth. For Wordsworth in

Title page of the *Chronicle of the Life of Elizabeth of Hungary* by Charles Forbes, Comte de Montalembert, 1835, translation by Ambrose Phillipps, 1839.

Illustration of
the Life of
Elizabeth of
Hungary, by
Edward Hauser,
1839.

those lines it was to be an intellectual regeneration, for Phillipps and his fellow Catholic Romantics it was actual. On 'Charnwood's forest ground' he built a house, Grace Dieu Manor, and a Cistercian monastery. Digby promised the profits of one volume of *Mores Catholici* towards the cost.

Later these buildings were altered or replaced by Pugin, whom Phillipps met in about 1836, and whose friend and patron he became. But the idea of Catholic Gothic architecture had preceded the fact of it. It was the patronage of such men as Phillipps that made it possible. They wanted these things before they found the man who could best accomplish them. Thus, though it would seem historically right that Pugin should have built the first rood-screen and the first monastery of the English Catholic Revival, the architect was in fact William Railton, whose best-known work is Nelson's Column. Phillipps's friend George Spencer, the younger son of the Earl, whose conversion in 1830 under Phillipps's influence caused a public sensation, also commissioned a Gothic church. This was built by Joseph Ireland at West Bromwich six years before Spencer met Pugin and commissioned another church from him.[31]

Like Digby, the younger generation of Romantic Catholic converts were cosmopolitan and in touch with the ideas arising from like minds on the Continent. Phillipps was much moved when he read, in serial form, the Comte de Montalembert's *Life of Elizabeth of Hungary*. Montalembert was a romantic antiquary, a campaigner with Victor Hugo for the restoration of the monuments destroyed in the Revolution. He had discovered the desecrated shrine of St Elizabeth at Marburg, and in one of those epiphanies to which the romantic temperament is liable, had been moved to rescue this sweet and lovely saint from the darkness of historical obscurity. His book, which went through numerous editions in France, tells the story of Elizabeth, a philanthropic noblewoman whose beloved husband is killed in the Crusades. It was illustrated by Edward Hauser, an artist of the Nazarene school.

The story was a perfect example of the ideals of Christian domestic life and marital love to which Ambrose and Laura Phillipps aspired. 'The most admirable and touching thing I ever read', Phillipps called it, finding many resemblances between the saint and 'my angel Laura'.[32] The Phillippses later incorporated the story of Elizabeth into the imagery of their private chapel in a window designed by Pugin.[33] Montalembert also identified the story with his own experience, dedicating his book to his sister Elizabeth, who had died at the age of 15.

Such a highly emotional, autobiographical religious faith was characteristic of the Catholic Gothic ideal. The romantic temperment found many opportunities for expression in medievalism, with its narrative tradition, its personal saints and portraits of donors participating in sacred events.

Phillipps translated *Elizabeth of Hungary* and attempted to dedicate his version to another virtuous young woman, Queen Victoria. The attempt was firmly and predictably snubbed. However, Montalembert and Phillipps came to know one another and through their friendship the ideas of François Rio reached Leicestershire.[34]

For Montalembert, the greatest Christian painters were Fra Angelico and Overbeck, leader of the Nazarene school. This view of art was one that Pugin came to share, as did his friend and fellow convert the artist J. R. Herbert.

In the similarities and the differences between Montalembert's and Phillipps's views the sensibility of Catholic Romanticism is summed up. Montalembert also saw Gothic art as 'la création la plus brillante de la foi'.[35] He, like Phillipps, had spent long months on picturesque pilgrimages among the mountains and ruins of Europe, wanderings punctuated by moments of epiphanic insight. Together he and Phillipps swore an oath, kneeling in the ruins of Fountains Abbey, on the site of the high altar, to restore the Catholic faith to England.

Yet, at the same time as they prayed for victory, what moved them was defeat. 'Je n'aime pas les causes victorieuses', Montalembert wrote.[36] The lost causes they chose to champion were, however, significantly different, for a certain distance was required to lend enchantment to the eye. Phillipps, like most of his Catholic convert contemporaries, dreamed of the restoration of the Bourbon monarchy. This irritated Montalembert, who had no illusions about the Bourbons and pointed out that among their faults was a total indifference to architecture. Montalembert for his part rose to the defence of Ireland, a suffering Catholic nation, whose poverty and piety moved him deeply. His support for O'Connell infuriated Phillipps, who thought, like many Englishmen, that 'no question was more misrepresented than the Irish one.' The French, he grumbled, 'make a MYTH of O'Connell'.[37]

For the moment the differences would not matter. The shared myth, the ideal of the quest was enough. Yet such incompatible elements as made up the Catholic Gothic Revival were bound, when the whirlwind that drew them together had passed, to separate again.

Montalembert, Phillipps, Spencer and Digby were among those whom Pugin found waiting to welcome him when he published *Contrasts*. There was one other, who was of great importance. The Earl of Shrewsbury, who became Pugin's greatest patron, was already a friend and sympathiser

John Talbot, 16th Earl of Shrewsbury, from the altarpiece formerly in the chapel of Alton Towers, Staffordshire.

of Phillipps. Shrewsbury was not a convert to Catholicism, yet he found himself, like the converts, in a position where a measure of self-invention was required. It was to the repertoire of *Waverley* and *The Broadstone of Honour* that he looked for it.

John Talbot was the 16th Earl but the first Catholic Talbot to be able to take his seat in the House of Lords, following Emancipation. After 1829 he felt called to play his unprecedented role as a Catholic nobleman in post-Reformation public life and did so with a mixture of flamboyance and austerity that fitted the chivalric image of the secular prince. His carriage, preceded by outriders on white horses, the splendour of his entertainments, these were due to the dignity of a Catholic earl. In his private apartments a deal table and coarse earthenware suited knightly simplicity. His frugality was not a pose, it was not insincere, but it was highly aestheticised.

The Armoury, Alton
Towers, Staffordshire:
Samuel Rayner,
*c.*1840

Shrewsbury's great house, Alton Towers, a magnificent
centre of English and indeed European Catholic society, was
a scene from *Ivanhoe.* A blind harper, Edward Jervis, played to
guests as they wandered among armour and stained glass
through the Gothic galleries. Here, as at Grace Dieu, before
there was a Pugin to employ, Shrewsbury had used more
ordinary architects, Thomas Fradgely, Robert Abraham and
Joseph Potter, to build the galleries and a chapel. Gothic
country houses were not of course peculiarly Catholic in the
1820s and 30s, but Shrewsbury certainly saw Catholic as
peculiarly Gothic. He had commissioned two Gothic
churches, St Peter and St Paul, Newport from Joseph Potter
and St John's, Banbury from Hickman and Derick.[38] Potter
was also building the new St Marie's College at Oscott, to

Oscott Chapel, Birmingham A. W. N. Pugin, 1837.

which Shrewsbury was a principal donor and where he would introduce Pugin.

For the present, however, while Phillipps, Montalembert and Shrewsbury were building, writing and campaigning, Pugin, their younger contemporary, was still an Anglican and, although an antiquary, not yet an architect. He seems to have known as little about the dawning Catholic Revival as he did of the Oxford Movement. Yet the notion of Gothic as Catholic hovered close to his own and his father's circle, for several of whom the study of medieval architecture was imbued with a romantic sense of its meta-physical, religious quality.

Design for a Catholic
Chapel by
A. W. N. Pugin, 1831
(*Victoria and Albert
Museum*).

One friend and collaborator of A. C. Pugin was Arcisse
de Caumont, a Normandy antiquary. In France secular antiquarianism had only a short history. It had arisen out of the
aftershocks of the Revolution, as English antiquarianism had
been born out of the Dissolution. De Caumont was one of
its principal begetters, as Montalembert acknowledged. To
De Caumont the expressive power of Gothic was self-evident. It embodied, unlike Classical architecture, not only
form but belief. These buildings, 'touchantes et ... religieuses',
were, De Caumont argued, forced yet further upwards by the
religious enthusiasm of the 13th century to the highest pitch
of Gothic perfection, when the intricacy of the carving came
to imitate the subtlety of thought itself.[39]

In Rouen, where the young Pugin went with his father and the other pupils of the family drawing school, he got to know Eustache-Hyacinthe Langlois, who became a lifelong friend. Langlois had accumulated a museum of antiquities which De Caumont thought 'marked an epoch', in French antiquarianism.[40]   But it was not only his collection that made a visit to Langlois remarkable. The museum was housed in the abandoned Convent of the Visitation of St Mary, among whose neglected cloisters and empty cells Langlois himself lived in a state of spectacular indigence, inhabiting his museum as Quasimodo inhabited Notre Dame.

In England, John Britton, also a collaborator with De Caumont and A. C. Pugin, was an imperturbable Protestant. In the great debate over nomenclature that exercised the English antiquaries of the 1820s and 30s, he seems to have taken from De Caumont the term 'Christian' for Gothic architecture. This suggestion was tentatively amended to 'Catholic' in 1831 by E. J. Willson in his introduction to A. C. Pugin's *Examples of Gothic Architecture*. Willson was the only Roman Catholic in A. C. Pugin's English circle.[41] The same year that Willson floated his idea, studiously ignored by Britton, A. W. N. Pugin made drawings for an imaginary Catholic chapel. It was the first time he used the word.

Five years later he wrote *Contrasts*. Within months of its publication Pugin was in touch with the Earl of Shrewsbury and through him with Phillipps, Montalembert and the others. This was the milieu from which most of his Catholic patronage would come and through which he would learn about the history of art outside England. He was welcomed by them as the hero of the hour and indeed it was an hour for heroes.

Half-a-century later, looking back on the tumult of the 1830s, John Henry Newman's brother-in-law Tom Mozley recalled: 'the whole fabric of English and indeed of European society, was trembling to the foundations ... a thousand projectors were screaming from a thousand platforms ... all England was dinned with philanthropy and revolution.'[42] 'In the story books of that date ...', he continued, 'the good man, the right man, and the true man, has only to show himself and to say a few words, and he carries all with him.'[43]

It was in this heady atmosphere that the few, passionate words of *Contrasts* were spoken and it seemed for a while that Pugin, the true man, would bring the greater truth of Catholic architecture to triumph. Little more than a decade later his moment had apparently all but passed. The reality of 19th-century Roman Catholicism let a bright, unsympathetic light in on the dream of the Middle Ages. Many, such as William Faber, who had been Goths and admirers of Pugin in their youth, changed their minds and saw it as a childish thing that should be put away. Faber became an Oratorian and one of Pugin's greatest opponents.

Thus the Catholic Romantic movement began to separate into its constituent parts. Those who remained within the Anglican church, loyal to the English Catholic tradition of Dugdale, valuing the connection between faith, history and architecture, were the Tractarians and Anglo-Catholics. They became Pugin's most consistent admirers but never of course fully his religious sympathisers. The Roman Catholic Church continued to build Gothic churches, as did every other denomination, including the Methodists, but for few, except Pugin's own son, Edward Welby, was this significant of more than the prevalent architectural taste of the time.

By the mid-1840s, the antiquarian tradition in which Pugin had grown up was also changing. For so long the province of amateurs and mavericks it was now increasingly academic, dominated by professional, university men who took a strictly scientific view of their work.

Pugin, disillusioned with the Church, though not the faith he had espoused, despaired before he died. He was already fatally ill when Newman preached the 'Second Spring' sermon and two months later he was dead. Lord Shrewsbury died within weeks of his architect and his heir outlived him by only four years. With the death of the 17th Earl, Alton Towers's Catholic days were over. Kerril Amherst, Bishop of Northampton, who remembered Alton in Shrewsbury and Pugin's time, went back in July 1875. 'To Alton', he wrote, 'poor old Alton. Lord Shrewsbury has established a turn-stile for excursionists to enter the grounds and gets threepence on every railway ticket.'[44]

Laborare est orare by J. H. Herbert, 1862 *(Tate Britain).*

Phillipps lived on until 1878. He remained a profoundly devout Catholic, although, like Montalembert, with whom his relationship became more distant, Phillipps grew increasingly liberal in his political views. When his father died, he moved out of Grace Dieu Manor in 1863. Later, when it was let it out to tenants, the chapel was shortened to widen the hall.

Only J. R. Herbert, in his paintings, kept the dream of Catholic England alive, though he and they outlived their day by several painful decades. When they were both old men Herbert used to visit Kenelm Digby at his house in Kensington. Yet even Digby came in the end to believe that Catholic truth had nothing to do with architecture. By the time he died, in 1880, his wife and four of his children had gone before him to lie in the chantry chapel at Pugin's church in Ramsgate. Digby decided not to follow them. For himself he chose a plain cross and a plot in the cemetery at Kensal Green.[45]

Acknowledgements
I am grateful to Professor Andrew Sanders for the loan of his copy of Milner's *Dissertation* and to Alexandrina Buchanan and Michael Hall for reading and commenting on the text.

Notes

1 From William Wordsworth, 'For a Seat in the Groves of Coleorton' (1811), *The Poems* (Middlesex, 1977), volume 1, p. 854.

2 John Henry Newman, 'Sermons Preached on Various Occasions', *The Works of John Henry Newman* (London, 1868-81), pp.168-89.

3 Quoted in Bernard Ward, *The Sequel to Catholic Emancipation* (London, 1915), volume 2, p. 88.

4 Quoted in Edmund Sheridan Purcell, *Life and Letters of Ambrose Phillipps de Lisle* (London, 1900), volume 1, p. 169.

5 Paul Frankl, *The Gothic: Literary Sources and Interpretations through Eight Centuries* (Princeton, 1960), p. 485.

6 Newman, op. cit. [note 2], pp. 168-9.

7 Graham Parry, *The Trophies of Time* (Oxford, 1995) gives an interesting account of the English antiquaries of the 17th century.

8 Walter Raleigh, *Historie of the World* (London, 1614), quoted as the epigraph in William Dugdale, *The History of St Paul's Cathedral in London* (London, 1656).

9 Parry, op. cit. [note 7], p. 232.

10 For a fuller account of the title page, see Parry, op. cit. [note 7], p. 231 and Margery Corbett, 'The Title-Page and Illustrations to the Monasticon Anglicanum, 1655-73', *Antiquaries Journal* (1986), pp. 102-9.

11 W. H. Oliver, *Prophets and Millennialists: the Uses of Biblical Prophecy in England from the 1790s to the 1840s* (Auckland and Oxford, 1978), p. 11.

12 Quoted in J. Mordaunt Crook, *John Carter and the Mind of the Gothic Revival* (London, 1995), p. 58.

13 John Milner, *The History Civil and Ecclesiastical and Survey of the Antiquities of Winchester* (2nd edition, London, 1809), volume 1, p. 15.

14 John Milner, *A Dissertation on the Modern Style of Altering Antient Cathedrals as Exemplified in the Cathedral of Salisbury* (London, 1798), p. viii.

15 John Milner, *Letters to a Prebendary* (London, 1800), p. 218.

16 Ibid., p. 216.

17 Op. cit. [note 13], volume 2, p. 32.

18 Op. cit. [note 14], p. 47.

19 John Milner, 'On the Rise and Progress of the Pointed Arch', *Essays on Gothic Architecture* (London, 1800), p. xvii, quoted in Frankl, op. cit. [note 5], p. 446.

20 Op. cit. [note 13], volume 2, p. 35.

21 Ibid., p. 241.

22 Ibid.

23 See in particular Peter Paul Bogan, *Beloved Chapel, the Story of the 'Old Chapel' of St Peter's Winchester* (Winchester, n.d.).

24 Op. cit. [note 13], volume 2, p. 241.

25 For an account of Digby's influence, see Mark Girouard, *The Return to Camelot, Chivalry and the English Gentleman* (New Haven and London, 1981), pp. 55ff.

26 Kenelm Henry Digby (editor Nicholas Dillen), *Maxims of Christian Chivalry from the Broadstone of Honour* (London, 3rd edition, 1926), p. 76.

27 Ibid.

28 Kenelm Digby, *Mores Catholici or Ages of Faith*, Book 2 (London, 1832), p. 265.

29 Ambrose Phillipps, letter to Laura Phillipps, June 24, 1835 (MS in private possession, microfilm in the Record Office for Leicestershire and Rutland, MF477). Stonyhurst is one of several Gothic Catholic works which fall outside the scope of this chapter but which are, in varying degrees, of relevance to its theme. Others include the chapel at Costessey Hall, Norfolk, 1809, and the Gothic reworking of the Catholic chapel in Stafford, both by Edward Jerningham; Holy Trinity, Newcastle under Lyme by James Egan, 1833 and St John, Tiverton by G. A. Boyce, 1836. Also of relevance is the non-Roman Catholic church of St Mary and St Nicholas, Littlemore, Oxfordshire, 1835 by H. J. Underwood and Hurrell Froude.

30 See above, note 1.

31 Ireland's church of St Michael was built in 1830-2 but rebuilt in 1876-7 by Dunn and Hansom. The church Pugin built for Spencer was Our Lady and St Thomas of Canterbury at Dudley, completed in 1842.

32 Ambrose Phillipps, letter to Laura Phillipps, May 29, 1836. [microfilm, as above, note 29].

33 The windows were designed in 1848-9, but not installed until after Pugin's death.

34 Rio (1798-1874) produced an entirely Catholic art history. His *Essai sur l'histoire de l'esprit humain dans l'antiquité, 1828-30* and *De l'art Chrétienne* (1841) argued that painting achieved its apogee in Fra Angelico and his contemporaries and that its spiritual power was destroyed with the Renaissance.

35 *Du Vandalisme en France, a letter addressed to Victor Hugo* (1833), collected in *Du Vandalisme et du Catholicisme dans l'art (fragmens) par le comte de Montalembert Pair de France* (Paris 1839), p. 2.

36 Mrs Oliphant, *Memoir of the Comte de Montalembert, Peer of France ... a Chapter of Recent French History* (London and Edinburgh, 1872), volume 1, p. 86.

37 Quoted in Purcell [op. cit., note 4], volume 2, p. 332.

38 John MacDuff Derick later became the architect of Pusey's church of St Saviour, Leeds (1842-5).

39 Arcisse de Caumont, *Cours d'antiquités monumentales* (Paris 1831), volume 4, p. 271.

40 Arcisse de Caumont, *Histoire Sommaire de l'architecture Religieuse, Civile et Militaire* (Paris,1830), p. 18.

41 A. Pugin, *Examples of Gothic Architecture* (London 1831-8), volume 1, p. xiv.

42 T. Mozley, *Reminiscences* (London 1882), volume 1, p. 272-4.

43 Ibid.

44 Mary Frances Roskell, *Francis Kerril Amherst DD* (London, 1903), pp. 316-17.

45 Bernard Holland, *Memoir of Kenelm Digby* (1919; reprinted Sevenoaks, 1992), p. 235 (cf. also a letter in the *Times Literary Supplement*, August 5, 1994, from Antony Tyler).

Appendices to Chapter 5

The Honble. Sr. Wm. Lee to Henry Keene Architect Dr: From 1752 to 1755. inclusive.

	£.s.d
Making a Design for a Church at Hartwell Bucks. Estimating &ca.for do: wth. Journey to Hartwl. & Expences attending Do. Making a Second Design in the Saxon Manner. several Journeys, & Expences attending do: to direct the several workmen in the Execution of do: the 2 above Articles – as p Agreement wth. Sr: Wm – 80 Guineas	84:0:0
To several Extraordinary drawings, Directions, & Journeys. occasion'd by Alterations, & Additions, to the Church &ca. more than was intended, at the making the above Agreement	16:0:0
	£100:0:0

Recd Novr: 21st. 1755 – The full Contents of this Bill
& all Demands p Henry Keene.

Dr: on Acct: of Moneys paid to the Several Workmen	£.s.d
To Mr. Booth Mason on Account	100:0:0
To Mr. Chapman Plumber do.	100:0:0
To Mr. Keene Senr. Joyner do.	200:0:0
	400:0:0

Recd. of Sr. Wm: on Account Oct. 25th. 1753 – £100. Mar. 6th. 1754 – £100.	200:0:0
	£200:0:0
To Interest of £200: for abt. 1 Year at 4. p Cent	008:0:0
Due on Ballance	208:0:0

Recd: Novr: 21st. 1755. the full Contents of the above
& all Demands p Henry Keene.

[verso]

Mr Keene	308: 0:0
Do Senr	90: 0:0
Glazier	43: 0:0
Chapman	42: 2:0
Stephen	14: 0:0
Dryhurst	76:10:0
Book	33: 0:0
	————
	611:10:0

[D/LE/D13/1]

Joyners Work done for Sr: William Lee Bart At Hartwell in Bucks
p Henry Keene

To the Altar all of Rt. Wainscot in the Saxon
manner the Moldings Composed of small unusual Members

	£ s d
67.11 Supl. on the face of In & 1/2 Rt. Wainscot plain back of Arches dov'taild on the back at 2s	6.15:10
56.0 of do. Circular on the Plan at 4s.	11: 4: 0
8.0 of Inch Wainscot Rebated Plinth at 1.3d	0:10: 0
2.8 of Do. Circular on the Plan in thickness at 5s.	0:13. 4
45.4 of In & 1/2 framing with hollow wrot. on Edge of do. and Inch & 1/2 Pannels at 2s.	5:13: 4
28.9 of do. to Gothick Arches with Circular molded hollows at 5s.	7. 3. 9
21.10 of Gothick Niches Vaneer'd in thicknesses on In 1/2 Wainscot with Molded hollow on Edge at 5s.	5. 9. 2
4.6.1/2 of Circulr Circular heads of Niches with framing as Niches Cut thro for Ornaments in thicknesses at 10s.	2: 5: 5
4.3 of In & 1/2 Wainscot pd. on 1 Side bottom of Niches at ls.6	0: 6:4 1/2
5.7 Cube of Wainscot prepd. for Carver for pinnacles &c at 12s.	3: 7: 0
19.4 Rung. of Cir.Cir Gothick Molding to Small Arches 2in & 1/2 Girt very Small Members in thicknesses at 2s	1:18: 8
17.10 of Do. and Circular on the Plan at 4s	3:11: 4
22.0 of Do. Cir Cir Molding to the Large Arches 8 In 1/2 Girt at 4s	4: 8: 0
9.8 of Strait Gothick Cornice 9" Girt at 2s.6	1: 4: 2
8.6 of do. Circular on the Plan at 5s:	2. 2. 6
32.3 of Cir.Cir rounds 3/4 Diamr in thicknesses at ls.6d	2: 8: 4 1/2
7.6 of Small Cir. Cir hollows wrot. on Edge of holes Cut for Ornamts in Arches. at 6d	0: 3: 9
8.6 of Caping under Flowers to the large Arches 10" Girt at 3s.6d	1: 9: 9
No.16 Columns with 2 Annulets & Base Moldings 5ft.7" high	

1 1/2 Diar at 7s.6   6. 0: 0
24 Ditto at Sides of Ditto 4 feet 2 Inches high with Annulets
and Base 3/4 diameter at 4s.   4:16: 0
12. Ditto with Annulets and Bases 5ft. 7" high 3/4 Diamr at 5s   3. 0: 0
20. Plinths to Groops of Columns Kanted in front at ls.6   1:10: 0
No.20 Capitals to the Columns 1" 1/2 diamr at 3s   4: 4: 0
6 Small Neck Moldings top of Small Arches at ls.6   0: 9: 0
6 Circular Do. on the Plan at 2s.6   0:15: 0
9 of Ornament Sunk in upper part of Arches at ls 6   0:13: 6
3 of Plinths under the Great Flowers Top of Arch at ls.6   0: 4: 6

                                                          _____

                                         Carried on   £82: 6: 9

No. 2 Pedestals in the Niches with Base & Impost 11 Ins. on
face and 9 Inches high with Ornamts. Sunk in Dado at 12s.   1: 4: 0
1 Ditto in the Center 1 ft. 4 on face & 9 Inches high at 15s.   0:15: 0
To the Communion Table with 6 Small Columns with Bases
& Caps Plinths and Arches, Sunk with hollow wrot. on Edge
Compleat   8: 8: 0
21.3 Supl. of Labr &. Nails to Bracketing back of Altar at 2d   0: 3: 6
5.5 Do. to Slit Caping at ld.   0: 0: 6

                                                          _____

                                         92:17: 9

The Pedestal Rail to the Altar
28.9 1/2 Supl. of Molded Base and Caping at 3s.   4: 6: 4 1/2
13.4 on 14 faces of Pedestals out of 2 In Wainscot ar 2s   1: 6: 8
10.0 Running of Small hollow wrot on Edge at 4d   0: 3: 4
4.8 of Circular Do. at 8d   0: 3: 1
20.4 Supl.of In 1/2 Wainscot pannels wrote both Sides of do.
at ls.8   1:13:10 1/2
No.34 Ornaments Cut thro' in do. and Sunk for Carver at ls Ea 1:14: 0
152.0 Running of Small Circular hollow wrot. on Edge of
do. at 6d   3:16: 0
52.0 of Circular rounds 1 3/4 Girt on do at ls   2:12: 0
Letting in 4 Iron Dogs to fasten do. to the Step   0: 2: 0

Making Molds for the Hinges and Latch	0: 4: 0
No.4 Iron Ts.& Ls. to fasten pannels	0: 6: 6
	——————
	16: 7:10

No.2 Desks for the Pulpit and Reading Desk with 2 large	
Columns and 6 Small do.with Bases Caps and Circular Arches and	
Wainscot Cornice and Desk Board Compleat at £7:10s Ea	15: 0: 0
Paid for painting ditto	0:12: 6
Making Molds for the Iron work to do. and putting it on	0:10: 0
	——————
	16: 2: 6

To the Outside doors Rt: Wainscot	
112.5 Supl. of 2 1/2 In framing and In:1/4 pannels with	
Molded hollow on framing to Gothick pannels on both	
Sides & Gothick heads with Letting in Bases & hinges	
& Rung. do. with Lead, and hanging	
Ditto (mead. on 1 face) at. 3s.6	19:13: 5 1/2
68.6 Running of Strait Molding on framing 3 Inches Girt at 9	2:11:4 1/2
37.6 of Circular do at ls.6	2:16: 3
69.6 of Strait Molds to Inside 2 1/2" Girt at 8d	2: 6: 4
31.6 of Circular do at ls.4	2: 2: 0
Making Molds for the Locks & hinges to do.	0: 7: 6
	——————
	29:16:11
	——————

	Carried on	£155: 5: 0

To the Pews in deal	
310.1 Supl..of In 1/2 deal framing with Inch pannels (mead. on	
face with Gothick Arches and Small Molded hollow on Edge	
and flush on the Inside at 10d	12:18: 5
2.7 of do. Circular on the plan at ls.6d	0: 3:10 1/2
64.0 of Molded Caping to midle pews and plinth at ls.	3: 4: 0
46.2 of Caping to front pews with Small Gothick Arches	
to Ditto at 2s	4:12: 4
104.8 Rung of Circular Circular Molding 3" 1/4 Girt	
to Arches at 9d	3:18: 6

No.57 Columns in fronts of pews 3ft. 3 high Including
Base Capitals and plinths at 2s:6   7: 2: 6
No.42 Roses prepared for Carving 4"1/2 Sqr. and fixing on
do. at 8d   1: 8: 0
No.4 Angle do. Rebated on the back at ls.4d   0: 5: 4
128.8 Supl of In 1/2 deal framg flush on both sides at 9d.   4:16: 6
6.11 of In 1/2 Wainscot Seat with Circular front at ls.6   0:10: 6
31.2 of whole deal plowed and tonged and Gleu'd to floor
of Desks at 10d   1: 6: 0
3.9 Cube of Oak Joists plaind and framd for do at 5s.6   1: 0: 7 1/2
51.1 Supl. of whole deal plaind on both Sides to Seat at 7d   1: 9: 9
22.6 of do. with Cutt fronts to Bearers at 9d   0:16:10 1/2

                                                                 _____

                                                                 43:13:2 1/2

Labr. and Nails only
33.0 of Steps and Risers with Molded fronts at 5d   0:14: 2
179.8 of Strait Joint Naild flooring & Oak Joists at 5d.   3:15: 0
1.11 Cubes of Oak plaind and framd to Support Desk at 2s.   0: 3:10
7.11 Supl.of whole deal plaind on 1 Side at 3d.   0: 2: 0
6.10 of Do. plain'd on both Sides at 6d   0: 3: 5
54.4 of Flush framing back of Seat at 5d   1: 2: 6
To putting on 4 Locks to the Pew doors at 8d   0: 2: 8

                                                                 _____

                                                                 6: 3: 7

To the Forms &c
85.0 Supl of whole deal Bearers with Cutt Edges at 9d   3: 3: 9
116.9 of do.Rail in front with do.at 10d   4:17: 3 1/2
247.0 of Inch & 1/2 deal plaind on both Sides with Molded
fronts to Seats at 9d   9: 5: 3
227.8 of Molded Ends and Backs at ls   11: 7: 8
103.4 of 2 Inch deal Ends with Molded fronts and Backs
Cut to Shape at ls:6   7:15: 0
No.320 Holes Cut in do.for Ornaments at 6d   8: 0: 0
580.0 feet Rung of Small Circular Hollow wrot. on Edge at 3d. 7: 5: 0
13.4 of Circular Moldgs on Edge Girt 2" at 6d.   0: 6: 8

                                                                 _____

                                                                 52: 0:7 1/2

                                                                 _____

Materials left occasiond by the Alteration of Pews but not fixt

19.4 Rung of Circular Circular deal Molding 3" 1/4 Girt.at 8d.0:12:101/2

8.6 Supl.of Molded plain Caping and Base at 10d   0: 7: 1

8.0 of Molded Caping with Gothick Arches at ls.9   0:14: 0

No.12 Columns 3ft.3 high Including Base and Caps &

plinths at 2s:3   1: 7: 0

No.8 Roses prepar'd for Carver at 8d   0: 5: 4

                                         _____

                                         3: 6: 31/2

To Sir William Lee's Gallery

27.10 Supl. of Couplets of Columns with Annulets and Base

in No.8 Columns at 3s   4: 3: 6

1.2 of do. Continued to the floor at 2s:6   0: 2:11

1.3 Cube of Fir prepared for Capitals at 6s.   0: 7: 6

51.5 Supl. of Gothick Groined Bracketing at 6d   1: 5: 81/2

9.9 of whole deal plaind on 1 Side at 5d.   0: 4: 1

6.7 of Cover board and Bearer at 6d.   0: 3: 31/2

44.6 of Deal Moldings at ls.   2: 4: 6

18.2 of Gothick Enricht Cornice with Small Arches and

Ornaments between ditto at 4s   3:12: 8

6.10 1/2 of 10 faces of Pedestals Sunk in front at ls.6d   0:10: 3

1.9 of Molded Ditto at ls.2   0: 2: 01/2

16.0 Run of Small Hollow wrot. on Edge at 2d   0: 2: 8

8.0 of Small Circular Do at 3d.   0: 2: 0

28.2 Supl. of 2 Inch deal plaind on both Sides at 10d.   1: 3: 6

No.44 Ornaments Cut thro' the pannels at 8d Ea   1: 9: 4

81.2 Run of Circular Small hollow wrot.on Edge at 3d.   1: 0: 3

                                         _____

                                         16:14:21/2

Ditto Labour & Nails only

113.9 Supl of Strait Joint Naild floor at 4d.   1:17:11

11.4 of Dov'taild Dado at 4d   0: 3: 9

133.0 of Flush framing at 5d   2:15: 5

70.1 of whole deal Seat planed both Sides and Clampt at 7d   2: 0:10

23.4 of Inch deal Skirting at 2d.	0: 3:10
34.11 of Moldings at 6d.	0:17: 5 1/2
16.6 of wh: deal 2 panl. doors at 5d.	0: 6:10 1/2
70.0 of Steps and Risers with Strings and bearers at 6d.	1:15: 0
4.4 Cube Fir planed and framd in Newells at ls.	0: 4: 4

£10:15: 5

Carried forwards £277: 2:11

To Altering the Pews Gallery floor 6 days at 3s	0:18: 0
756 Feet Supl. of whole deal packing Cases fit for flooring and other uses including packing and unpacking Ditto and Clearing Nails &c at 5d ft.	15:15:0
To 3 Joyners 12 days going from London to Heartwell and Coming back again	1:16: 0

28:14: 5

£305:17: 4

Measured Sept: 16th: 1755 pr: Jn Harris.
November ye 21 1755 Recd: of the Right Honrabl Sr Wm: Lee the Sum of ninty pounds the Remainder of this Bill being in full for the above Bill p me
Henry Keene

[D/LE/D13/3]

Plumbers work done for the Honble: Sr Wm Lee Bart. at Hartwell
Church - Bucks p Wm: Chapman p Order of Mr Henry Keene Architect.
From June 1753 To Sepr: 1754 –   £ s d

29:3:27: of Lead us'd in the Gutters, at 17s p lb	25: 9:10
56:2:19 of Do. to the 2 Towers - hips of roof, trap	
Doors &ca:–deld: after the rise of Lead at 20s.	56:13: 4
0:2:25 of Sodder to the whole at 9d p lb	3: 0: 9
144 Feet 8in: of Gothic Pipe made in 3 shafts at 3s:6d	25: 6: 4
24 feet of 4 1/2 In plain Do bottom Lengths at 3s p ft.	3:12: –
4 Gothic Cistron Heads & Labour to make do at 25s ea	5: –: –
54 Feet of Plain 3in 1/2 pipe to bring water from Tower flats &	
Sockets to do at 2s.6d p ft.	6:15:–0
1 Gross of Screws & 8d & 4d Clout Nails to the whole	1:14: 6
Paid a Carpenters bill for Packing Cases	3: 1:10 1/2
Paid Carriage of the whole to Hartwell to Inn 0:18:6	
by Rogers 5:10:0	6: 8: 6
Two Plumbers 37 Days Each to lay the Gutters, Flats &ca:,	
and to fix up the Pipes, Cistern Heads &ca & going &	
returning at 3s p day	11: 2: –

                                                 ─────────

                                                 £147: 4: 1 1/2

Novr. 21 1755
Recd the full Contents of this bill and all Demands pr Wm Chapman

[D/LE/D13/4]

Masons work done for the Honble: Sr: Wm Lee Bart: at Hartwell Church
Bucks – p Thos: Booth p order of Mr Henry Keene Architect – £ s d

127:4 Run: of Portland stone Coping to Towers 15in. wide, 5in thick, & Coins to do included at 2s:9d – p Ft. run:	17:10: 2
137:8 Run: of Cornice do: 21in: wide, & Coinstones to do: included at 3s:6d p ft	24: 1:10
227:8 Run: of Large Cornice to Building 2F:6I wide, & Coins to Angles & Buttresses included at 6s:3d p ft. –	71: 2:11
Paid Mr Rogers for Carriage of the whole –	21: 2: –
	£133:16:11

Measd: &ca: Augst: 26th: 1755
Recd. the 21st. of Novr. 1755 the Contents in full of this Bill
& all Demands p Thos. Booth

[D/LE/D13/5]

The Honble Sr: William Lee Bart Dr. To James Dryhurst for Carving done
to A Rich Gothick Altarpiece in Wainscott at Hartwell Church near
Ailsbury
Bucks by the Order of Mr Keen Surveyor
1754 Decb 5   £ s d

	£ s d
For 6 whole Leafs to Pediment	3: 6: 0
For 12 half Leafs to Do	3: 6: 0
For 12 Raffled Leafs to Do	2:10: 0
For Spandall Roses on both Sides	4: 4: 0
For 10 Pinnacles	20: 0: 0
For 3 Double Tops of Leafs to Pediment	9: 0: 0
For 6 Capitals	2: 8: 0
For 4 whole Gothick Capitals & 4 3Qur ones to Do	7:10: 0
For 7 Roses in the Deal Gallery	1:10: 6
For the Pulpit & Reading Desk in Deal	
For 8 Trusses Scroles Leafs & Ivy Leafs	5:10: 0
For 4 Spandals in the pannells wth Ivy Leafs & berries	5:10: 0
For 4 3Qr: Capitals 2 1/2 In High	2: 0: 0
For 9 foot large Cavetto in Wainscott Gothick Arch & Roses	
a 6s/6d	2:18: 6
For 2 Raffled Leafs to Ditto	0: 8: 0
For 54 Gothick Roses in Deal 4 In Diamr a 2s/9d each	7: 8: 6
For 32 Gothick Roses 2 In Diamr a 1/3 each	2: 0: 0

£79: 9: 6

November the 21 1755 Recd: the full Contents of this Bill &
all Demands Thos: Dryhurst

[D/LE/D13/6]

The Honble. Sir Wm: Lee for Hartwell Church p order Mr Keene
Architect To Thomas Stephens Dr.

£ s d

1755 Mar 10th
To 3 Extra Good & Strong Rim Locks home made & twice
dead in Suit with wards full & round & 3 keys & Strong Brass
Plates on the key hole of the Caps Screwd. & 3 Scutns. with
Large drops on the Outside Plates of ditto   4:10 -
To 3 Extra Large Scutns & Drops & 18 fine Screws & 9
Extra Strong 2 1/2 Inch ditto   6 -
To a Machine Brass Latch for an Alter rail with a Mortis Ring
handle & Bevil to Pattern wth a Strig. Plate & Six fine Screws   5 -

April 15th
To. 4 pr. Strong Pew hinges holes Counters sunk   12 -
To. 7 Doz Inch 1/4 Screws   3. 6
To.3 pr Center hinges for the Outside doors of ye Church the
Bearing Pins Turnd. & Steeld. & all Turnd. Caps & Countersunk 3. 2. 6
To 8 1/2 Doz Strong 2 Inch Screws   12: 9
25 To 4.5 Inch Iron Rim Locks in Suit for Pew doors with
high fronts & a Slyding Bolt Screws & Staples &ct. Compleat
& Varnisht wth 6 keys   1.14 -

May 15th
To. 2 Cranes pained & Turned with Spring Latches in Ditto &
Stops & Dovetails to go into the Wall for the Pulpit &ct.   1:16: 0
To. 2 Round Barrs to ditto wth Dovetail ends & Screwd.   18. -
To 4 Bevil Straps for ditto & 3 1/2 Doz Screws   1. 9
19 To fitting the Plates for the Pulpit door frame to the
wood at Mr. Keenes Shop   9

July 8th
To 1 pr. Double Joynted hinges made to Pattern for the Alter
Smooth filed   10 -
To 2 1/2 Doz In' 1/4 Screws   1: 3

Aug 25th

To a new Plate & Scutn. for the Lock of the Church door   3. -

To Turning the Center & Pin of the Joynts of the hings: to
make them the other hand   2. 7

        £14.18. 6

Recd: Novr: 21: 1755. The full Contents of the Bill & all Demands
pr Thos Stephens

[D/LE/D13/7]

Glazier's Work done for Sr: Wm. Lee by Wm. Cobbett
1755 Augst. 2d   £ s d.

743 ft.: 3In. Sup Crown Glass in broad lead, cutt in Gothic Figures
cemented & at 14d p foot   43: 7: 1 1/2

A Man 8 days going & returning twice   1 - -

Paid for the Packing Cases &   1:15: -
                                                      _____

                                                        46: 2:1 1/2
                                                      _____

                                                         3: 1:11

                                                        43: 0: 6

NB: the Carriage, will be charg'd by the Carrier to Sr. Wm. Lee
1755 Novr. 21st Recd. the full Contents of this Bill and all Demands
p Willm. Cobbett

[D/LE/D13/8]

The Honble: Sr Wm Lee Debter to Edward Haines
Octber: 3 1754

	£ s d.
144 Crocketes on ye Pinikells at 2s. 6d pr	18:00: 0
12 Portland finishing to dito at 8s: pr	04:16: 0
5 finishing Over ye windows at 8s pr	02:00: 0
4 Large Roses at 10s pr	02:00: 0
2 Over ye Cansell window at 3s pr	00:06: 0
12 Under ye windows at ls pr	00:12: 0
4 Blank shields at 4s pr	00:01: 4
1 Bear	00:07: 6
4 Coates of Armes	04:00: 0

£32:02:10

Recd: in Part of this bill   £10:10: 0

£21:12:10

Recd: ye full Contents of this Bill and Demands by me
Edward Haines

[D/LE/D13/9]

August 22D. 1754 A Bill of Masons work done for the Use of the Honble Sr. Wm: Lee for Building a new Church at Hartwell pr Wm. Bolland Jno Gibson

	£: S: D
9631 feet of plain Ashlour done of Wadden Hill Stone at 6D. pr foot work only	240:15:6
3320 feet of Molding work Do at 9D pr foot	124:10:0
3321ft: 6 In feet of Totternhoe Stone molding in the Windows Cornish String Corses Do at ls:6D pr foot Stone and work	249: 2:3
971ft: 5 In feet of plain Circular Molding to the Aytick windows and Upper windows in the Towers at ls: pr foot	48:11:5
143:9 feet of plain Totternhoe stone at 9D per foot	5: 7:9 1/2
Rods:Q ft 37: 1: 21 to Chapping the Stone for the inside walls at £1:1s:0D pr Rod	39: 4:0
71:0:0 to the foundations and inside walls reduc'd to the Standard at £1:1s:0D: pr Rod	74:11:0
5:3:13 to the Brick Groins at £1:10s:0D. pr Rod	8:14:0
1105 ft: 7 In of Chap'd Circular work to Recesis of windows &c at 4D pr foot	18: 8:6
To letting in 75 Doz 2 Cramps at ls pr Doz	3:15:2

To Cutting and leading 208 holes to plug the open work
together atop of the Towers at lD pr hole   0:17:4

To Cutting and leading 132 holes to plug the
Pyremids to gether at 1. 1/2D pr hole   0:16:6

                                                                            _____

                                                                            £814:13:5

                                               whereof paid   682. 0.0

                                                                            _____

                              remains due on this account   132:13:5 1/2

October 13th 1755
Recd: of Sr W: Lee the sum of one Hundred
& thirty two pounds thirteen shillings being
the Ballance due upon this account pr: _____
Wm Bolland   £132.13.0

                                                                            _____

[D/LE/D13/11]

Stucco work done for Sr: William Lee Bart: at Hartwell Church
p Thos: Roberts

The great Stucco Cieling to the body of ye
Church done down to top of the Capitals,
compleatly finished with Gothick Moldings
and ornaments   £ 250:0:0

No 8 Large Columns Consisting of several
shafts with Enrich'd double Capitals, plain Bases
and double Annulits: at £7 Each   56:0:0

8 Circular windows with plain Moldings &
Coves at £2 Each   16:0:0

4 Large windows with 2 Columns to Each
Enrich'd Caps, plain coves round ye windows,
OG Arches to the heads, ornamented with
moldings & foliage leaves at £8:10 Each   34: 0: 0

2 Compartments over Doors for Inscription
Tables Ornamented as the windows at £7 Each   14: 0: 0

2 Large Arches to openings to Altar & Gallery,
ye work the same as ye windows, with sofits
wrot: in many Gothick pannels at £11 Each   22: 0: 0

The Groins under Gallery with Moldings &
ornaments   7: 0: 0

A Gothick Cornice to Gallery   4: 0: 0

The Chancel Cieling compleatly finished with
Gothick Moldings & Ornaments   63: 0: 0

4 Columns to Angles with their Caps & Bases
at £5 Each   20: 0: 0

2 Circular windows	3. 0: 0

2 ornamented Arches to window & opening at
£6 Each   12 0 0

The Ground work of all the walls to ye body
of ye Church Chancel, and Gallery done with
Trowil'd Stucco and Scaffolding to the whole   75:0:0
                                                              _____

                                                              576:0:0

NB All the Ornaments and Moldings are cast in Solid Alabaster, and all
the Lime Bristol, which is Included into the above prices
For plain Stucco to the Walls to the Porch down at the House, and
Colouring the walls in the Hall £3:10:0

[D/LE/D13/12]

Hartwell Church

140 feet of gothick Coping on Battlements And Buttress's at 1/2s 3d	£15.7.0
Do. Round Towa 112 at 2s	11:4:0
Pinicles on Church & Towers at 4s.4d. Each	50. 0 0
Pillasters to Tower – from Coping to Cornsh at 5:5 Each	42. 0. 0
Portland Coping to Plinth round the Church About 200 foot at ls:5d:	£11:13: 0
	193:12 0

[D/LE/D13/22]

General Abstract of Bills of work done for the Honble. Sr. Wm. Lee at
Hartwell Church Bucks. by the London Tradesmen by ye. Architect.

	Bill	Money pd. on Acct.	Due
Mr. Henry Keene Senr. Joyner	305:17:4	200:0.0	105.17.4
Mr. Wm. Chapman Plumber	147. 4.1 1/2	100:0:0	47: 4:1 1/2
Mr. Thos. Booth Portland Mason	133:16:11	100:0:0	33:16:11
Mr. Thos. Dryhurst Carver	79: 9: 6		79: 9: 6
Mr. Thos. Stevens Ironmonger	14: 8: 6		14: 8: 6
Mr. Wm. Cobbett Glazier	46: 2: 1 1/2		46: 2: 1 1/2
	——————	——————	——————
	726:18: 6	400:0:0	
	400		
	——————		
Ballance Due			326:18: 6

[D/LE/D13/2]

Notes on the authors

Dr Alexandrina Buchanan is Archivist at The Clothworkers' Company. Her doctoral research was on the architectural historian Robert Willis (1800-1875) and the study of Gothic architecture. She has published numerous articles on contemporary and later attitudes to medieval architecture and is currently working on a study of architectural terminology. Her articles include: 'The Power and the Glory: Medieval Architecture and Meaning', in I. Borden and D. Dunster (editors), *Architecture and the Sites of History: Interpretations of Buildings and Cities* (London, 1995); '"The science of rubbish": Robert Willis and the contribution of architectural history', in Frank Salmon (editor), *Gothic and the Gothic Revival. Papers from the 26th annual symposium of the Society of Architectural Historians of Great Britain* (Manchester, 1998); 'Science and Sensibility: Architectural Antiquarianism in the Early Nineteenth Century', in L. Peltz and M. Myrone (editors), *Producing the Past: Aspects of Antiquarian Culture and Practice 1700-1850* (London, 1999); 'John Bilson and the "Domical" Vaults of Anjou', in *British Archaeological Association Conference Transactions*, 2000.

Dr Terry Friedman, retired Principal Keeper of Leeds City Art Gallery and the Henry Moore Centre for the Study of Sculpture, is the author of *James Gibbs* (1984) and *Church Architecture in Leeds 1700-1799* (1997) and numerous articles on the designing and building of Georgian churches. He is currently researching and writing a book on this neglected subject.

Michael Hall is the Deputy Editor of *Country Life*. His most recent book is a history of Waddesdon Manor, published in 2002. He is currently working on a study of the architects Bodley and Garner.

Rosemary Hill is a writer and historian currently working on a biography of A. W. N. Pugin. Her recent articles include: 'Reformation to Millennium: Pugin's *Contrasts* in the

History of English Thought', *Journal of the Society of Architectural Historians* (March 1999), and 'Pugin and Ruskin', *British Art Journal* (Summer 2001).

Maurice Howard is Professor of Art History at the University of Sussex. He is the author of *The Early Tudor Country House* (1987), *The Tudor Image* (1995) and a forthcoming co-authored book on the The Vyne, Hampshire, covering the first, Tudor, 16th century phase of its archaeology history.

Dr Timothy Mowl is a lecturer in the Department of History of Art at Bristol University, where he specialises in architectural history and landscape design. He is Co-Director of the department's MA in Garden History. In the garden history field he has published *Gentlemen & Players - Gardeners of the English Landscape* (2000) *and Historic Gardens of Gloucestershire* (2002), the first of a Pevsner-type series on the historic gardens of the Engish counties; Dorset will appear in 2003, to be followed by Wiltshire in 2004 and Oxfordshire in 2005. His last study in architectural history was a polemical analysis of 20th-century attitudes towards architecture and conservation entitled *Stylistic Cold Wars - Betjeman versus Pevsner* (2000). His chapter in the present book relates to an earlier publication, co-written with Brian Earnshaw, *Architecture Without Kings - the Rise of Puritan Classicism Under Cromwell* (1995).

Dr Giles Worsley is architecture critic of the *Daily Telegraph* and former architectural editor of *Country Life*. His more recent publications include *Classical Architecture in Britain: the Heroic Age* (1995) and *England's Lost Houses* (2002). He is a fellow of the Society of Antiquaries and of the Royal Historical Society.

Index

(entries in brackets refer to illustrations)